CAMBRIDGE LIBRARY COLLECTION

Books of enduring scholarly value

Travel and Exploration

The history of travel writing dates back to the Bible, Caesar, the Vikings and the Crusaders, and its many themes include war, trade, science and recreation. Explorers from Columbus to Cook charted lands not previously visited by Western travellers, and were followed by merchants, missionaries, and colonists, who wrote accounts of their experiences. The development of steam power in the nineteenth century provided opportunities for increasing numbers of 'ordinary' people to travel further, more economically, and more safely, and resulted in great enthusiasm for travel writing among the reading public. Works included in this series range from first-hand descriptions of previously unrecorded places, to literary accounts of the strange habits of foreigners, to examples of the burgeoning numbers of guidebooks produced to satisfy the needs of a new kind of traveller - the tourist.

Biographical Memoir of James Dinwiddie

This is an account of the career of James Dinwiddie (1746–1815). First published in 1868 by Dinwiddie's grandson William Jardine Proudfoot, the work is based on Dinwiddie's own autobiographical notes, travel logbook and personal correspondence. The biography traces Dinwiddie's career from the scientific lectures he gave from 1781 and the journal series *Queries and Hints*, which he began in 1779, to his visit to the Chinese imperial court as official astronomer in Lord Macartney's mission (1792–4); his residence in Beijing and Canton; and his move to India, where he was appointed Professor of Mathematics, Natural Philosophy and Chemistry at the College of Fort William, Bengal. Dinwiddie's career was marked by passionate commitment to the dissemination of scientific knowledge – his travels, lectures and publications were undertaken for this cause. His life is a fascinating account of a polymathic mind which will fascinate and entertain a modern-day readership.

T0382589

Cambridge University Press has long been a pioneer in the reissuing of out-of-print titles from its own backlist, producing digital reprints of books that are still sought after by scholars and students but could not be reprinted economically using traditional technology. The Cambridge Library Collection extends this activity to a wider range of books which are still of importance to researchers and professionals, either for the source material they contain, or as landmarks in the history of their academic discipline.

Drawing from the world-renowned collections in the Cambridge University Library, and guided by the advice of experts in each subject area, Cambridge University Press is using state-of-the-art scanning machines in its own Printing House to capture the content of each book selected for inclusion. The files are processed to give a consistently clear, crisp image, and the books finished to the high quality standard for which the Press is recognised around the world. The latest print-on-demand technology ensures that the books will remain available indefinitely, and that orders for single or multiple copies can quickly be supplied.

The Cambridge Library Collection will bring back to life books of enduring scholarly value (including out-of-copyright works originally issued by other publishers) across a wide range of disciplines in the humanities and social sciences and in science and technology.

Biographical
Memoir of
James Dinwiddie

*Astronomer in the British Embassy to China,
1792, '3, '4, Afterwards Professor of Natural
Philosophy in the College of Fort William,
Bengal*

WILLIAM JARDINE PROUDFOOT

CAMBRIDGE
UNIVERSITY PRESS

CAMBRIDGE UNIVERSITY PRESS

Cambridge, New York, Melbourne, Madrid, Cape Town, Singapore,
São Paolo, Delhi, Dubai, Tokyo

Published in the United States of America by Cambridge University Press, New York

www.cambridge.org
Information on this title: www.cambridge.org/9781108013796

© in this compilation Cambridge University Press 2010

This edition first published 1868
This digitally printed version 2010

ISBN 978-1-108-01379-6 Paperback

BIOGRAPHICAL MEMOIR

OF

JAMES DINWIDDIE, LL.D.

BIOGRAPHICAL MEMOIR

OF

JAMES DINWIDDIE, LL.D.,

ASTRONOMER IN THE BRITISH EMBASSY TO CHINA, 1792, '3, '4:

AFTERWARDS

PROFESSOR OF NATURAL PHILOSOPHY IN THE COLLEGE OF

FORT WILLIAM, BENGAL:

EMBRACING

SOME ACCOUNT OF HIS TRAVELS IN CHINA
AND RESIDENCE IN INDIA.

Compiled from his Notes and Correspondence by his Grandson,

WILLIAM JARDINE PROUDFOOT.

LIVERPOOL

EDWARD HOWELL, 26 CHURCH STREET.

1868.

TO THE READER.

NATURAL science is unquestionably one of the grandest subjects of human investigation. The pursuits of literature or the fine arts, however pleasing in themselves, fall short in comparison of the sublime truths unfolded by the material universe. Whether soaring into illimitable space, or descending the scale of nature to view the world of wonders displayed in a single drop of stagnant water, the mind becomes everywhere stored with rich and exalted ideas, and loses those narrow prejudices which but too frequently arise from local habits or a contracted education. The man on whom this study has its due influence receives the clearest insight into the problem of his own existence. He considers himself as a citizen of the world, and looks upon every man, of whatever country, color, or creed, with the most impartial eye; he cannot, in fact, but be a good man.

Curiosity, the principal motive to this study, is more or less in the minds of all men; but it is so implanted in some as to abstract them from every other pursuit, and engage them in intellectual researches by a thirst after knowledge which no discovery can quench—which success inflames the more. When Descartes had taken a survey of all the employments of men, in order to choose a profession, he became persuaded that he could not do better than devote his whole life to investigating the truth. The value, however, of any character does not depend so much on what a man knows, but what he can do. Knowledge which terminates in itself is but an amusement; at the same time it is the amusement most becoming a man—a gentleman—one who has had the advantage of a liberal education, and, as such, must be classed among the luxuries of life. But science has a close connexion with life; it mingles in all the arts, is the foundation of many, and contributes to the improvement of all; and these objects ought to be considered as the great end of the study of natural philosophy.

The career of James Dinwiddie is a singular instance of devotion to science. Born in a humble sphere, with only his own perseverance to carry him forward in the world, he stemmed the torrents of an adverse fortune till he became the most popular lecturer of the day. For variety and extent of learning he was believed to have been unsurpassed; but little, however, is known of him beyond that he spent a long and active life in diffusing the knowledge he had accumulated. That the memory of such an individual should pass away with his generation has been often regretted by his friends, and to trace his career is the object of the following Memoir, which is attempted to be drawn from his manuscripts and correspondence alone. It is rather unfortunate that so much time has elapsed, and that these papers, which are the only sources of information, are often so effaced or mutilated as to afford little or no assistance whatever in elucidating the subject in view; and how far this compilation will bear out the observations hazarded above will depend on the judgment of a discerning reader.

W. J. P.

CONTENTS.

𝕭𝖎𝖔𝖌𝖗𝖆𝖕𝖍𝖎𝖈𝖆𝖑 𝕸𝖊𝖒𝖔𝖎𝖗

OF

JAMES DINWIDDIE, LL.D.

CHAPTER I.

EARLY LIFE, ETC.

THE individual whose life is here attempted to be traced derives his descent from ancestors long settled in the parish of Tinwald, near Dumfries. In this parish the farm of Kirkland had been in the occupation of the family from an early period in the life of his great-grandfather. The name was originally spelt Dinwoody, or Dinwoodie, which the Doctor, when a very young man, modernized as it is written upon the title page. His parents, John Dinwoody and Catharine Riddick, were humble, and cultivated the small farm already mentioned. They had five children, three sons and two daughters, all born on the premises.* The subject of the following Memoir, their youngest child, came into the world an orphan on the 8th December, 1746, more than half a year after the father had been consigned to his grave. The eldest son was then but twelve years old, and a heavy burden devolved upon an industrious mother, who was exceedingly interested in the welfare of her youngest child. So soon as he was able the orphan James had to take a share in the duties of the farm, by looking after the cattle, and such other tasks as suited his tender years. A neighboring village supplied the first rudiments of learning, but the system of education pursued at small country schools is seldom calculated to " teach the young idea how to shoot." There no interesting object draws the attention, while a dull sameness prevails that leaves but too much room for indolence or idle pursuits. However first directed, it is certain, at a very early age, a curiosity for mechanical contrivances was the ruling passion of James Dinwiddie's mind. The consequence was, the cattle under his charge were frequently committing trespass while he was busy employed upon his favorite schemes. The shop of the village wheelwright, from which he had been often beaten for neglected duties, presented objects far more

* The names of the children were respectively, Margaret, William, John, Jean, and James.

B

congenial to his feelings than manœuvreing with cattle. Some remarkable instances of his early ingenuity are still on record, but the best authenticated memorial was a wooden clock, made entirely by his own hands, which not only kept time well, but was long regarded as a curiosity in the neighbourhood, even by himself after he had risen to distinction. When a boy he was exceedingly timid, and had an unfortunate squint in the left eye; but these circumstances only increased the bias of his friends, who, eventually, deemed it prudent to bestow on him a good education. The humble industrious classes in Scotland frequently furnish instances of individuals liberally educated for some of the more learned professions, which, in most cases, is that of a clergyman. Such was the object contemplated by the relations of young Dinwiddie, who had the lot to be born in a family strongly attached to the principles of the national church. He was sent to the Dumfries academy, which, at this period, had acquired considerable reputation from the ability of its teachers. Here the youthful aspirant to knowledge commenced the study of mathematics and the languages, and laid in a good foundation, to be completed afterwards at the University of Edinburgh.

Although designed for the church, his favourite study was science, to which he became irrecoverably rivetted by the lectures of Professor Robison and others in the Scottish metropolis. When the necessary preparations to fit him for the pulpit had been gone through, and after having delivered his maiden sermon before the Presbytery, to the disappointment of his friends, he refused to become a preacher, and gave himself up entirely to science. His first dependence upon his own exertions for support was as tutor to the families of Collin and Arbigland, in Galloway; next as teacher and session's clerk to the town of Port Glasgow, from whence he removed, in November, 1771, to superintend the mathematical department of the academy at Dumfries, where he became the associate of those distinguished teachers, Waite, Chapman, and Butterworth.* To the usual duties of a mathematical teacher, the attention of the pupils was invited to occasional short lectures on natural and experimental philosophy; and not unfrequently to an excursion in the fields to learn practically the use of the instruments

---

* Besides his able colleagues, this academy could boast of many men distinguished as clergymen, or in other learned professions. Among them, too, was John Anderson, a merchant, who afterwards settled at Cork, where he acquired a princely fortune, and, during the troublesome times of the Irish rebellion, rendered Government such essential aid in carrying the mail, that the honour of knighthood was offered him. Though declined by the father, the honour was accepted by the son.

employed in surveying, levelling, navigation, &c. He thus grew a favorite in the school-room, and was much respected by the community at large. As an evidence of the distinction he had already acquired, the Edinburgh almanack of this period mentions upon its title-page, " The calculations by Mr. James Dinwiddie, mathematician, Dumfries." His philosophical researches continued to be pursued with the most untiring industry, and he became so great an enthusiast that he often filled his head at the expense of a hungry stomach. Effects and their causes formed the grand hinge upon which his enquiries turned. To promote his views, he was the means of instituting a philosophical debating society among the literati of the place, which was carried on with spirit for several years. He had also the honour to establish the first course of public lectures on natural philosophy in his native town, as he styles Dumfries. These lectures, which were delivered at intervals during the whole of a winter season, at once raised his philosophical standard in the south of Scotland. On the subject of mechanics, we find him introducing the clock he had made when a boy. This piece of early ingenuity was removed from his mother's house on purpose, and its place supplied with another of the common eight-day construction.

CHAPTER II.

CAREER AS A PUBLIC LECTURER.

IN February, 1778, the University of Edinburgh conferred on Mr. Dinwiddie the distinction of Master of Arts. His passion, however, for philosophical studies had by this time involved him in embarrassment. The first cost of his apparatus plunged him at once into a debt of one hundred and fifty pounds, to pay off which the only scheme, that carried probability of success, was that of giving public lectures. The indulgence of the magistrates and council of Dumfries enabled him to put this into execution, and the approbation of his friends encouraged him to go on. Among the list of Mr. Dinwiddie's approvers occurs the name of Professor Dugald Stewart, who writes him an invitation to give them some instruction in Ayr. Leave of absence was asked but for a limited period, as he still retained the control of the academy, where he placed an assistant to take the immediate charge till his return. Thus prepared, he set out, in the summer of 1778, to amuse the learned, and instruct those who do not fall under this denomination, by a set of lectures on natural philosophy, assisted by a powerful train of experiments.

Bending his steps to the north, his expectations were fully realised, particularly at Edinburgh, Leith, and Dundee. In the spring of the following year he made a successful tour through Galloway, and, contrary to advice received from most respectable authority, as a peculiarly unfortunate period, passed over into Ireland, on the 18th July. To transport the apparatus it was imperative to freight a small vessel, which, on reaching the Irish coast, could not, from the low state of the water, proceed directly to Belfast, its destination. Mr. Dinwiddie and two fellow travellers deemed it advisable to lose no time in getting ashore at the village of Holywood, where, finding no mode of conveyance, they walked a distance of four miles to Belfast, which they reached at a late hour. They had been recommended to one of the principal hotels in the place, yet, instead of meeting with that attention their appearance as gentlemen demanded, they found accommodations altogether inferior. This trifling incident, in connexion with former advice, impressed Mr. Dinwiddie, at the moment, with an unfavorable opinion of his new adventures; but on seeking an explanation the following morning, the reason was found to arise from the circumstance of the gentlemen arriving *on foot.* " So much," as Mr. Dinwiddie observes, " was this antient and simple mode of travelling despised." However, he had no reason to regret his visit to Belfast, which became the first scene of his operations in the sister island. His name had been there before him, and the encouragement he received confirmed him in his views of making the tour of that kingdom. The encouragement, indeed, occupied nearly three months, while Lisburn, Newry, and Drogheda, further delayed his progress to Dublin, where he arrived on the last day of January, 1780. His arrival at the capital had been looked for with great impatience by his friends. During a space of five months several courses were delivered, and though he does not speak so favorably of his reception here as in the north, room still seemed to exist for future lectures. Having finished his engagements, he sailed June 26th, for Cork, and landed July 10th, still followed by success.

To show the manner in which Mr. Dinwiddie treated the subject, and also how earnest were his endeavors to draw the attention to useful and practical applications of science, the subjoined extracts are taken from the observations preliminary to a course on natural philosophy.

" Having given you an account of the way by which we acquire a knowledge of nature, it now remains to lay down the method I am to pursue in the following lectures.

" We investigate the mechanical properties of natural bodies by means of observations made on the mechanical appearances of nature. These mechanical appearances are changes of motion, and these changes of motion are the only immediate objects of our observation, and must be understood before we make any inference of the cause that produced them. Now, in the account already given, we saw that the cause was an inference from phenomena. Phenomena, then, must be understood before we can arrive at the cause, and it is evident any error in our notions of the phenomena must give rise to error in the notions we form of the cause. I shall therefore begin with giving you some account of motion.

" This will naturally lead me to make some observations on time and space, in which every motion must be performed. I shall then give you some notion of matter: that is, I shall ascertain what are these characteristical properties which distinguish it. On this subject, I shall confine myself to its mechanical properties. Philosophy treats of events in the mechanical world. Events are changes in the state of things. Without these changes philosophy never could have had a place among men ; all our knowledge would have been confined to natural history. But such changes are observed, particularly changes of motion. We see these changes continually and uniformly attending the impulse and approach of bodies, hence we conclude that the cause of these motions reside in the bodies. Thus are bodies related by carrying along with them the cause of changes in other individuals.

" The laws of nature respecting these changes are two-fold ; they are necessary and contingent. I shall first consider the necessary laws of motion.

" Our disquisitions on these subjects will be the most abstract and difficult in the whole course. We must dwell chiefly on general ideas, as we can seldom descend to single instances on account of the differences to be found in every individual. This, however, I shall always do when it is in my power, in order to show you that specific differences do not affect the general conclusion. But though it be difficult it has also its advantages. It may lead to conclusions we could not otherwise arrive at, and it will not fail to render our subsequent investigations far shorter and more perspicuous than they could otherwise have been. But it possesses still greater advantages than these. Mechanical philosophy will thus be considered as a demonstrative science. Were we to rely solely on observation and experiment, we would still, in some degree, be liable to inaccuracy and error ; but this will become demonstrative if we build only on obvious principles, and propositions that are self-evident, and, in our application of these, adhere steadily to the rules of sound logic. This branch of the course, in which I am to consider these mechanical properties, I call *dynamics*.

" Aided by these general data, I shall here examine all the variety of mechanical phenomena which nature exhibits, in order to explain their properties, and to explain subordinate events. Having finished these two subjects, I shall give a mechanical history of *body*.

" In this history I shall begin with the most general, and then descend to those of smaller extent. Now the most general of any is the curvilineal motions of bodies in free space. Of this we have examples in all the bodies in the solar system. Thus *physical astronomy* will form the first article of this mechanical history.

" The careful observer of phenomena will observe another general property of matter, which is called *gravitation*, and which he considers as belonging to every particle that exists in the universe. Having discovered its existence, and ascertained its power in the more general motions, we may then apply our knowledge to explain subordinate phenomena, as for instance, the ebbing and flowing of the tides, the irregularity of the earth's motion, and many others ; and we may then apply it to the articles of astronomical calculations, gunnery, and dialling.

" Thus will we gain all the ends of philosophical research, first to investigate the principles, explain subordinate phenomena, and improve the arts.

" From the known fact that the moon follows the earth in her motions, we infer *gravitation* between the moon and the earth ; so from the fact that when I move one part of my body every other particle follows it, we infer the power of *cohesion*. I call it a power as it is an effect that produces motion.

" Having made this inference of *cohesion*, which is only an effect, we may proceed to examine its nature, to consider the appearances which characterize its nature, which is various in bodies that are hard, soft, or fluid.

" We may still observe other phenomena that are similar to what takes place in this of cohesion. These are considered as indications of another power which is called *elasticity*. This is manifest in solid bodies, which, when they are either stretched or compressed always, regain their original form. It is most sensible in air. These also may be called by the general name of *corpuscular force*. This *corpuscular force*, however modified, is the cause of the firmness of solids : of the communication of motion ; of motion among the particles of matter ; of impulse. It is the cause of the chemical phenomena of solution, precipitation, effervesence, chrystallization ; it is the cause of vegetable and animal secretion, and assimilation.

" In treating of this subject I have *first* to ascertain the mechanical properties of this power by the observation of phenomena.

" 2.—I shall explain the phenomena which are the consequence of its exertion, and here I shall confine myself to these consequences which are immediate, and most easily investigated. I shall consider the firmness of solid elastic bodies, and on this part of the subject various maxims will occur which will be of use to the engineer ; and here too I shall take an opportunity of explaining the principles of the ancient artillery.

" *The second branch* shall treat of the communication of motion in solid bodies, where first we shall treat of bodies as elastic or non-elastic, or what is called the doctrine of collision and impulse.

" 2.—The communication of motion by means of the intervention of other bodies. In this will be included the theory of mechanics, and we shall take occasion to make some remarks on friction, and the piercing of solid bodies, as in ploughing, driving poles, the impression made by shot and shells, and some other circumstances.

" *The third branch of corpuscular force* will contain the mechanics of fluid bodies, wherein *first* we will treat of the properties of those generally called liquids. This part of the course is called *hydrostatics*, in which we consider the pressure arising from gravitation, or any other cause, and examine the laws which regulate the distribution of this pressure. This may be applied to the construction of dams, of locks upon canals ; it may also extend to the mechanism of floating bodies, to ship-building as it regards stowage and stability in the water. We shall *then* treat of fluid bodies. In this we shall explain the method of conducting water by canals or pipes, of water mills, and of ship-building, as it regards the quickness of the motion and obedience to the helm. This part may be called *hydraulics*.

" *Hydrostatics* and *hydraulics*, then, comprehend the mechanism of fluid bodies, which are called liquid. But of fluid bodies there are others of an aërial or elastic kind, of which *air* is the chief. Here we shall inquire into the mechanical motion of sound, and give you a mechanical theory of music. This science, when applied to improve art, considers the structure of wind-mills, the working of ships, and several other articles.

" Besides *air* there are some other fluids which resemble air in this distinguishing property of elasticity, as *steam*, which gives rise to the fire engine.* So also *gunpowder*, which produces its effects

---

* Steam engines were then called fire engines.

from the elasticity it acquires in expansion when it is rendered fluid. This will lead us to explain the use of gunpowder in artillery or in mines.

" *The fourth branch of corpuscular force* treats of the internal motions of the particles of bodies, as in the motions which take place in chrystallization, fermentation, precipitation, &c., and in animal and vegetable secretion and assimilation, though on this subject I shall only point out the particular attempts that have been made to explain them, and lay down some rules to enable you to judge of these attempts.

" Having thus considered the more general properties of bodies, I shall next consider those phenomena which are less general, viz., the phenomena of *electricity* and *magnetism;* and then, in the last place, the phenomena of the perception of objects by our sense of seeing. This is *optics*, and the last branch of our course.

" Thus have I given you a sketch of the various articles of which we are to treat, and shown you that the principle of our arrangement is the generality of the phenomena. In the process of our investigations on these subjects, it is plain that we must often have recourse to mathematical reasoning where the train of argument is always perfect, and where the belief is irresistible. But were we to proceed in our inquiries only by the aid of the abstract sciences, the objects of research would frequently be apprehended with difficulty, and be apt to elude the view. Some method then must be fallen on in order to render the task of attention easy, and to give a more lively idea of the subjects of discussion. This is done by means of an experiment, which, although only a single and detached fact, yet, as it is susceptible of examination by the senses, conveys a stronger and more perfect impression than if all were left to the exertions of imagination. A very simple instance will illustrate this truth. Any one will, undoubtedly, by a single glance of the eye receive a more clear and distinct idea of the figure of this room, and of the relative situation of the different objects in it, than what he could receive from the most accurate and elaborate description.

" Such then is the study of mechanical philosophy, and such the branches of knowledge to be acquired in the prosecution of it. The account I have given will, I hope, preclude the necessity of spending much time in enumerating the advantages that attend the study of it. Indeed, it needs no panegyric. The utility of the science evidently appears from the intimate connexion it has with all the arts. To some it gives rise and is useful to all. But not to the arts alone does it lend its aid. To the student of jurisprudence it holds forth many advantages. In many cases respecting the decision of property this science is the surest guide, and innumerable are the instances where injury has been the result of ignorance. Had judges in general been better acquainted with its principles, we would not have found the annals of every country, and of every age, stained with the blood of so many sorcerers. How often, too, do we find the historian introducing miraculous affairs into his relations, and filling his work with fable and absurdity. Those who have persued the histories of Herodotus, Livy, and some other such as those, will seek no other proof of this assertion. The most unspeakable advantages accrue from this study to the physician ; nay, so intimate is the connection between them that natural philosophy and medicine have got the same name. Indeed I may be allowed, without being suspected of partiality, to assert its utility to the physician, when I see every day theories drawn from this subject, and, supported by the greatest names, introduced into medicine continually, and I see them as continually abused. As to those who are engaged in a course of study, with a view to be the religious instructors of mankind, it is needless to recommend this science. So essential has it been thought to them that it has been appointed as a necessary branch of their education, and, in my opinion, it ought to be considered as something more than a mere embellishment to the theologian.

" Such are some of the advantages that the study of this science will always afford. But besides these it possesses many others, for I will be bold to assert that that method which now begins to characterize the other sciences, is mostly owing to the use of mathematical science which first acquired credit here, and viewing it in this light, we may consider it as paving the way to a spirit of general inquiry.

" In this science, too, we meet with many new and unexpected discoveries which, by their novelty, surprise and astonish us. But accustomed to this we begin by degrees to be less astonished, and feel comparatively little surprise at any discovery, however new or however inexplicable it may appear. This gives rise to a sober and rational scepticism, and we soon find our happiness improved by the maxims we learn from the study of nature. In this study, too, is formed the surest foundations of a rational theology. The ingenious mind, although well aware that the field upon which it has entered is immense and unbounded, yet so far is he from feeling pain at this, that he prosecutes with double ardour a journey where every step he advances presents a new pleasure, and which he is conscious will never have an end.

" Thus have I given you an account of the task imposed upon me by my office. The study of nature, I confess, has always to myself afforded singular pleasure, and I may be allowed without fallacy to assure you that it is with the greatest satisfaction I devote my labours to your improvement in this science. I shall be glad to hear of your improvement in any department of philosophy, but here I shall have the peculiar happiness to think that I have contributed to this end. But to secure success I must solicit your assistance. Knowledge and zeal in any public teacher are not of themselves sufficient. The young philosopher must hear with candour, attention, and patience, and after all I cannot pretend by this course to teach you natural philosophy. I can only direct the course for your future studies. The field is extensive, but time will not allow us to travel over it. Our journey of consequence must be hasty, and many objects, even of importance, viewed only with a passing glance. But to accommodate such as have not the advantage of mathematical knowledge, I shall leave all mathematical investigations that are any how tedious and difficult to the evening lecture. Though the use of that hour is chiefly for mathematical demonstration, yet, in order to save time, I shall occupy the first three weeks in giving you an account at the hands of physical astronomy, as there is no particular institution where this is peculiarly attended to."

On another occasion the importance of geometry to natural science is thus enforced :

" I know that of late an opinion has been allowed to gain ground that a complete knowledge of natural philosophy may be acquired without mathematics. But this is the language of those who, having no mathematical knowledge themselves, cannot be admitted as competent judges. I appeal to fact. It is only in those parts of the science which have been mathematically considered, that natural philosophy can boast of having carried on her investigations with certainty, success, and utility. Many think themselves natural philosophers because they are in the habit of making experiments in electricity, chemistry, &c. This is very laudable, and by such labours the science will in proper hands advance ; but I would desire you to remember that these gentlemen are either natural historians employed in collecting facts, and perhaps arranging them in such a manner as may enable the man of true science to investigate their true causes ; or they are employed in chemistry, physiology, or such other branches of the general study of nature, where as yet we contend ourselves with the discovery of causes, and where the immediate cause of the phenomena is out of the question. When the chemists made their collection of the chemical laws of solution, precipitation and so on, they were either natural historians, or contented with joining together events whose relation was remote; but when Sir Isaac Newton attempted to investigate the immediate cause, and consider that power which occasioned the effervesence in a mixture of chalk and aquafortis, he found himself obliged to proceed on the properties of quantity. When Dr. Black pointed out a variety of double exchanges, and arranged them in a convenient order, he was only a natural historian; but when he came to investigate the immediate cause, and assert the nature of the power which produces the double exchange, he was obliged to employ the property of number and figure. In short, gentlemen, without a moderate share of mathematical knowledge, you can expect only a schoolboy's acquaintance with natural philosophy, resembling those religionists who take up their authority on the opinion of their priests, and neither can give a reason for what they think they believe, nor apply it to any good purpose in life. Without a moderate share of mathematical knowledge, you may read the flimsy and indeterminate writings of a Nollett or a Priestly, but you cannot profit by the truths delivered by a De Lambert or a Newton."

Regular but shorter courses were also given in various branches of natural history, on chemistry, and on the fine arts, and, occasionally, separate single lectures on a great variety of subjects, such as fortification, gunnery, the diving bell, aerostation, pyrotechny, &c. Mechanics furnished a fair quota of subjects, particularly machinery, in which improvements, suggested by himself, were introduced. Wheel carriages formed a favourite subject; but to the general audience the most interesting of these single lectures was one devoted to a ship. He says: " Whether we consider its immense size, the vast load which it carries, the ease and velocity with which it is moved, or its great utility to mankind, we must be convinced that a ship is by far the noblest machine that has ever been invented by man. Let us try, if possible, to divest ourselves for a moment of our present experience: let us suppose we have never observed any body floating on water, and that a man comes into this company who declares that, on a certain occasion, he saw a building of wood, more than two hundred feet long, and about fifty feet broad, floating on the surface of the water, carrying about one thousand inhabitants, flying at the rate of ten miles an hour: that a single man could change its direction; that he saw it lay its broadside to a city, and in a few hours reduce it to ashes. What credit could be given to such a relation? How different is the estimate we form of the works either of nature or of art when we consider them as single detached facts, and when we trace them through the various steps according to which they have arrived at their present pitch of improvement."

Two years had now elapsed and terminated the period granted for Mr. Dinwiddie's absence, when the authorities of Dumfries became anxious for his return, which various circumstances conspired to prevent. His success had been much greater than he had reason to expect from his little experience, and want of that confidence so necessary for pushing on through the world. He, however, soon found that, to please the giddy and unthinking, who compose the greater part of every audience, as well as the necessity of carrying his lectures to a degree of perfection equal to any of his predecessors or contemporaries, considerable additions to the apparatus were necessary from time to time. His ambition to excel in his favourite study swelled with the apparatus, and he had now advanced so far as to find it impossible to retreat. His connexion with the academy being, latterly, only nominal, and of no longer service either to himself or the town of Dumfries, he gave in his resignation, with grateful acknowledgments for the favours received.

To avoid unnecessary expense in transporting the apparatus from place to place, the disposition of the inhabitants were previously sounded through the correspondence of his acquired friends. He was always well recommended by letters of introduction, which seldom failed to procure him ample acquaintance wherever he went. Though still somewhat diffident in public, the bashfulness of youth had so far disappeared that he was become very partial to the society of his friends, which included naval and military officers, engineers, architects, millwrights, mathematical instrument makers, medical gentlemen, teachers, &c. A mind forcibly impelled by philosophical inquiry naturally seeks the company of intelligent men of every description, where, in the course of friendly conversation, new ideas are often started, and much information brought to light. His company was, besides general conversation, much courted for *facetiæ*, all which not unfrequently led him into clubs, assemblies, and private parties; and the necessity of supporting a respectable appearance, added to his professional expenses, was a constant draught upon his means. Mr. Dinwiddie had never studied economy, and was further from it than ever in Ireland, where the reward of his labours was spent with a lavish hand, and but too frequently allowed to be embezzled by a young relative who accompanied him in the capacity of assistant and collector. Fortune so far had crowned his endeavors with a smile, which the fickle dame was about to change into a frown. A second course of lectures at Cork, where the first was well received, proved a complete failure, and his intentions of visiting Limerick met with a decided negative. To improve particularly the lectures on fortification and gunnery, he had just increased the apparatus by expensive models of a fort, town, and camp, together with the line of battle at sea, and a variety of warlike implements, including some brass cannon cast on purpose. His funds were then at a very low ebb, and the only alternative was to hasten back to Dublin, the means of doing which he expected to realise at Kilkenny, which lay directly on his route, and where a tolerable subscription appeared to await his arrival. To his utter astonishment, however, but five subscribers came forth, and these were dismissed after a few experiments in electricity. For the first time he was entirely without funds and a single intimate acquaintance, and daily increasing in debt, which he wished to keep secret. How to get himself, his assistant, and baggage to Dublin, was now beyond comprehension. Taking courage to unfold his embarrassment to one of the subscribers, that gentleman kindly advanced him five guineas, and in the space of a few hours fortune seemed to smile again by introducing a fellow-traveller proceeding to the capital. The stranger, correctly no doubt, assumed to be a merchant in Portugal, and just arrived from Cork, where he landed. It was a very happy meeting, and arrangements were made to travel together in a chaise to start early in the morning. In the evening, however, an accident discovered both to be in the same awkward predicament—without sufficient funds. The discovery is interesting, and strikingly illustrative of the benevolent disposition of Mr. Dinwiddie. A young lady, also anxious to reach Dublin, but without money, had learned what was transpiring, and made her case known to the philosopher, begging in the most earnest manner to be taken along. Mr. Dinwiddie was extremely willing to assist her, but could give no guarantee without consulting his fellow-traveller, who was then absent. That gentleman, on his return, rejected the proposal as most unreasonable. A little later the lady made her re-appearance, expecting to find matters in her favour, and was thunderstruck when informed that the merchant could not be prevailed on to give his consent. At this she redoubled her entreaties, which made such an impression on Mr. Dinwiddie that he resolved on making another trial; but it was of no avail. He then frankly informed his fellow-traveller that he (Mr. D.) was without sufficient money, otherwise the question would not have been urged a second time. This announcement completely paralysed the merchant, who pleaded being in a similar difficulty as the only grounds of his objection. In short, each had calculated to borrow from the other, on the way, the necessary expenses to complete the journey. The lady, of necessity, was left behind, but the gentlemen started agreeably to their appointment, and reached their destination in the evening of the second day, with rather empty stomachs and otherwise put about.

The curiosity manifested by Mr. Dinwiddie's former visit had in a great measure died away, and he by no means experienced the attention anticipated. The additional arrangements in fortification, &c., proved a serious disappointment, particularly in regard to the military, on whose patronage great reliance had been placed. His affairs in a short time became so embarrassed that he would have disposed of the apparatus could a purchaser have been found at any thing like a reasonable price, but, unwilling to sacrifice it, kept struggling on to little purpose. Towards the summer of 1781 his prospects brightened somewhat in the north, where he had many admirers, at whose desire he commenced a campaign which occupied about half a year. His principal engagement was at the Institution, Belfast; but other places in the province were successfully visited, and on one occasion he had the honor of lecturing before the Lord Bishop of Down as his patron. By this venture, he was enabled to return to Dublin with nearly a hundred pounds in his pocket, clear of all expences. But a generous and unsuspecting disposition rendered Mr. Dinwiddie an easy prey to designing men, and, unfortunately, one, who had always professed the greatest friendship, contrived to borrow the money, and immediately became bankrupt. The absolute want of money in a strange land is a position not to be envied, and it assuredly required no little fortitude to bear up against the current of disappointments that now seemed to have set in. After a variety of schemes to extricate himself he fortunately got a job to teach geography, and some other learned branches, at an academy in the vicinity, to which he agreed to walk two days in the week. The progress of the scholars gave every satisfaction to their friends, and proved the harbinger of better days, by drawing a greater amount of attention to the lecture room in the city. At the academy, an engagement, which lasted two years, was subsequently entered into, and necessarily confined Mr. Dinwiddie to Dublin, from whence he seems only to have ventured in a single course delivered at Waterford.

Among a variety of new incidental subjects, which continued to to be tried with varying success, the celebrated Woolwich Foundry formed an important lecture. These works were explained from a model, an expensive purchase by Mr. Dinwiddie, to whom money was no object when anything new or extraordinary presented itself. It is described in the syllabus as " A large and elegant model of the Royal Foundry at Woolwich, containing the furnace, boring engine, and every instrument necessary for the casting, boring, and finishing of cannon, mortars, and howitzers; and including a bell foundry. The whole constructed by the King's late celebrated founder, Van Bruggam, and from which model the present foundry was built."

The famous siege of Gibraltar, from a model too, was attended with some degree of interest among the higher classes. But a more thrilling subject was the Line of Battle at Sea. After describing the chase, and subsequent preparation for action, with a minuteness that could only have been ascertained from anxious inquiry, he says: " The thunder of the artillery; the harsh cracking of the musketry; dismounting cannon; cutting to pieces the fall of masts, yards, and sails; the groans of the wounded and dying—all conspire to produce a scene of which we landsmen can form but a very imperfect idea. In the midst of all this, to possess the mind calm and undisturbed; to give out orders clear and without confusion; to take advantage of every shift of the wind, or oversight of the enemy—favorable moments of occasion which are rapid in their flight and never return—is a task for which few individuals are equal. Yet such have commanded; such do command; and such I hope ever will command the fleets of the British Empire."

The 2nd of June, 1783, proved fatal to Mr. Spalding, the celebrated improver of the diving bell. This gentleman's successful efforts had robbed diving of its terrors so completely that it was quite a common occurrence to be accompanied by his friends wishing to visit the bottom of the deep. Among those occasions wherein he had signalized himself was the wreck of the Royal George, from which he had raised seventeen guns. At the time of his death, he was, with an assistant, engaged upon the wreck of the Belgioso, East Indiaman, sunk on the Kish Banks, about eighteen miles from Dublin. A fatal concurrence of circumstances disarranged the position of the bell, and prevented the signals from giving information above. When drawn up the men were both dead. This accident was widely lamented, and by none more than Mr. Dinwiddie, who exerted himself in tracing the unfortunate cause, upon which he delivered several successive lectures to large audiences, all anxious to hear the explanation. The particulars were ever afterwards embodied in the discourses on the diving bell, which, though in a lecture-room, was at this time sufficiently extensive to admit a diver inside. Mr. Dinwiddie had on some previous occasion attended Mr. Spalding in his operations, and had just made arrangements, upset by this fatal event, to descend with an air pump, and some other apparatus, to try experiments in condensed air, particularly relating to sound, tune, and concord.

In the process of diving, "the bell is slung from the yard-arm, bowsprit, or any other part of the ship properly secured. The diver goes into the boat, and when the bell comes near the surface of the water he takes his seat. The first thing remarkable is the great increase of sound in the bell; the diver startles at his own voice, and a gentle tap is like the blow of a mallet. The bell should be let down slowly, followed by a barrel of air at eight or ten feet. The diver now begins to feel a pain in his ears, which increases as he descends. At twenty-five or thirty feet the pain is excessive, and sometimes occasions a discharge of blood from the ears. At about thirty-three feet the diver feels a sudden shock, or crack in the ears, which is alarming at the first experiment; but instead of the tympanum of the ear being broken as he suspects, he finds the pain instantly removed, and is perfectly at his ease. The pressure of the condensed air in the bell, against the drum of the ear, occasions the pain. There is a communication between the mouth and the cavity behind the tympanum, by means of what anatomists call the eustachian tube. When the air in the bell, and consequently in the mouth of the diver, arrives at a certain degree of condensation, it forces open this tube, rushes in behind the tympanum, and becomes a counter-balance for the pressure on the outside. The tympanum is by this means reduced to its natural state, and the pain consequently removed. Whatever length of time the diver remains at this depth, he feels no more of the pain; but if he descends deeper it is renewed, and at about sixty-six feet a second shock takes place. There is generally light enough for the divers to do any work. The cold at the bottom is disagreeable, but this may be remedied by lapping several folds of flannel round that part of the body immersed. It is prudent never to turn the stop cock, except when the barrel of fresh air is at hand to supply the place of that let out."

With all his efforts, Mr. Dinwiddie's prospects continued to be deeply overcast, and he heartily wished for a change. A strong invitation had been received from America, but he laboured in vain to throw off the meshes in which he was entangled. In July he became still deeper involved by attempting to follow out the speculation of saving a part of the Belgioso's cargo. For this purpose a small vessel and a number of divers were engaged to go upon the wreck, and prosecute his plans. But soon after the operations had commenced, he left Dublin, and crossed the channel for England. His departure was so sudden that many of his intimate friends knew nothing of his intentions. The Philosophical Society of Manchester, of which he was a member, was about to be organised by the appointment of a number of professors, and it is presumed that he had got intimation thereof. It is certain he took Manchester in his way, and was offered the chair of natural philosophy and chemistry, which he would have accepted had the encouragement been equal to his wishes. His present system of lecturing, however precarious the profits might be, was nevertheless sufficiently alluring to set aside the appointment now offered. The field was wider, and hope still seemed to point towards more successful times. London had never yet been tried, and another object of this tour was unquestionably to sound the channel of success there, and, if possible, pave the way for future adventures. Although accompanied by a very small portion of his apparatus, Liverpool, Manchester, Sheffield, &c., were visited in a professional capacity; at the same time, advantage was taken of the opportunity to examine the different manufactures of those places, with a view to future lectures.

At this period, attention throughout Europe was first roused by the news of the air balloons, in which, shortly afterwards, Blanchard and others began to mount into the atmosphere, trusting themselves to the mercy of the winds in so untried and flimsy-like a piece of mechanism. Ere yet, however, such ascents had been attempted, at least in this country, the sight of an air balloon was eagerly desired, and the interest thus manifested was turned to account by Mr. Dinwiddie, who, soon after arriving in London, was busily engaged in constructing one about 15 feet in diameter, With the constructing business he pretends to have been better acquainted than any man in England, having made a peculiar discovery which rendered the silk perfectly air-tight. This brought him various commissions to execute for private gentlemen. But whether the metropolis favored his views is not once mentioned; he, however, collected a little more apparatus, and with his balloon found ample encouragement to extend his tour through the South and West, visiting particulary Bath, Bristol, Exeter, Portsmouth, Southampton, and Winchester. Such was the popular desire to see an air balloon that, when at Exeter, an hour was appointed for the exhibition which interfered with some public business, a requisition was got up to have the experiment delayed, so as to afford every citizen an opportunity of witnessing the same. In different parts of the country similar balloons were occasionally seen floating through the atmosphere, causing consternation sometimes to simple-minded people. When launched, it was difficult to say where the voyage would end. While tracing out his own, Mr. Dinwiddie encountered some strange adventures, and in

c

one instance the obstinacy of the captors would not so much as permit it to be seen until forced by the strong arm of the law.

Fully twelvemonths had elapsed when the channel was re-crossed, by way of Bristol and Waterford. During his absence from Dublin little or no correspondence had been kept up, and the greater part of his friends there had almost despaired of seeing him again. He was in fact so remiss a correspondent that he seldom took the trouble of writing, even when his own interests demanded it ; and it was almost a miracle that the apparatus was not disposed of before his return by the owner of the lecture room, to whom in particular he was under considerable obligations for rent. Somehow or other he was tempted to write a friend an account of his balloon adventures, and of his intention of re-visiting Ireland in the same capacity, which had the effect of inducing the party, who had the control of the instruments, to hold out a little longer and wait his return.

Attention, in Ireland, was quite as much absorbed in the balloon mania as it had been in England. On resuming his labors in Dublin, Mr. Dinwiddie—many of whose experiments were original—contrived a new and beautiful one to give his audience a good idea of an aërial voyage. A small bladder, two or three inches in diameter, was blown nearly full of air, and covered with a thin net of common thread. To the lower part of the net was suspended a gallery or triumphal car, in which were two figures representing the aërial travellers. The whole was made just to sink in a tall jar of water laid on the plate of the air pump, and covered with the guinea and feather, or fountain receiver. On working the pump the balloon rose, and again descended on letting in a little air. The least motion of the handle and stop-cock produced the effect, and matters were so adjusted as to conceal this motion, which gave the balloon the appearance of ascending and descending by word of command.

Soon after his return to Dublin, offers were made to transport himself and apparatus to settle in Russia, under Prince Potemkin, who had got a grant from his government of a large tract of country, into which he was extremely solicitous to introduce the arts and manufactures of more enlightened nations. Colonel Bentham, the chief promoter in this enterprize, believed the knowledge of Mr. Dinwiddie would be valuable in assisting the Prince to carry out his favorite schemes. When first communicated, Mr. Dinwiddie was disposed to embrace the offer, but his mind was in a continual vortex of speculation, and he had read the letter so carelessly as to be under the impression that his destination would be in the neighbourhood of St. Petersburg. On receiving more definite information—that it would be in the Crimea—he thought no more of it. The splendour and populousness of the Russian capital seems to have inspired him with expectations not to be realized from the rude and thinly inhabited tracts of the Crimea.

Mr. Dinwiddie continued to struggle with difficulties until confinement to Dublin preyed seriously on his mind. The grand obstacle to a change was the apparatus, which he could neither redeem nor dispose of, unless at a greatly reduced price. Seeing no prospect of freeing himself, and unwilling to remain longer in this hopeless condition, he resolved to leave, even without the instruments, which were arranged to remain in the possession of his landlord, but subject to the supervision of a young relative, who had been the close companion of his travels, and who was now about to settle in Dublin. Mr. Dinwiddie did not despair of being able, sooner or later, to pay their ransom, and under this impression, early in 1786, commenced his journey to the north. At Belfast he had the full command of the apparatus appertaining to the Institution, and which was once more brought into requisition. From Belfast he passed over into Scotland, after an absence of seven years. Conflicting accounts of his progress and success had circulated here from time to time, and his return was hailed by his early admirers as the termination of his travels. All along he had been a very negligent correspondent, arising mainly from the multiplicity of his engagements; yet the silence with which he treated some of his best friends awakened in him many bitter reflections. But for transitory accounts occasionally found in a newspaper, his very existence had been held in dispute; and letters not unfrequently came to hand with only his name and the ample range of Ireland for his address. Although weary for a permanent location, yet his wandering habits were equally confirmed in his own country, into which he landed by way of the Clyde. A flattering reception awaited him at Port Glasgow, from whence he went direct to Edinburgh, where he was enabled to increase his small stock of instruments by the addition of such others as would be adequate to a full course of lectures. Finding the field clear, he made a tolerably successful tour, visiting most of the important towns as far north as Aberdeen. In all his travels no opportunity was ever lost of acquiring information connected with arts and manufactures and improvements in machinery. This tour was particularly taken advantage of; and the spinning mills of Glasgow and Dundee, the iron works at Falkirk, and the tar works at Culcross, are enumerated among those that drew his attention.

Scotland had strong attractions, but fame and fortune seemed only linked with the capital of England, into which he at last resolved to throw his fate, sink or swim. He was now unwilling to lose time, particularly as inquiries had been made after him by two foreign gentlemen there, the Marquis Del Campo, Ambassador from the Court of Spain, and a Doctor Luzuriago. The Marquis had written to his Court respecting Mr. Dinwiddie, and had offers to make concerning an appointment in some foreign expedition. Mr. Dinwiddie was naturally anxious in regard to the issue of these inquiries. Towards the end of February, the year following his arrival in Scotland, and without once visiting the place of his nativity, he sailed from Leith and landed in London, pursued by ill health and bitter disappointments. The object of the Spaniards remains a mystery, but gloomy as his prospects were, he seems to have preferred them to the offers of the foreigners. What proved the severest trial was the irrecoverable loss of the most valuable portion of his apparatus, which untoward circumstances had compelled him to leave behind in Dublin. The individual under whose direction it was placed was a relative on whom the most indulging favors had been lavished; yet to him much blame is attached for allowing the instruments to be sacrificed to suit some selfish end. To replace them now was the most serious consideration. In London Mr. Dinwiddie had few friends, and success in such a place was not to be expected with a trifling apparatus. His friends about the Scottish capital were more than ever ardent in their endeavors to induce him to return, and set up an academy there. The declining state of Professor Robison's health was looked upon as a favorable circumstance, and Mr. Dinwiddie seems to have approved of the measure, but was unwilling to leave London without a trial, particularly during the sitting of Parliament. Clouded as his own prospects were he was still in a position to render essential service to a Scottish friend, and his benevolent endeavors were not exerted without their reward. With a little pecuniary assistance from that quarter, and an intimate acquaintance with some of the London philosophical instrument makers, he was enabled to fit up a lecture room, which turned to so good a purpose that he gave up the idea of returning to Scotland. In procuring apparatus, he regrets disposing of the model of a cotton machine, which, during his late residence in the north, he had constructed at a deal of trouble and expense, and on which he set a high value.

Vexatious clouds continued for a time to cross the atmosphere of his ambition, yet eventually Mr. Dinwiddie was not much mistaken in his calculations regarding London. A course suitable for Sunday evenings was highly approved of. It was striking into something new, and making his name more generally known. In the course of two years his prospects wore so bright an aspect that he expresses himself, in a letter to a friend, as now getting into the line which all along had been the object of his aspirations. Every exertion was strained in keeping up his growing popularity. The love of novelty is a useful and powerful ingredient in the constitution of the human mind, of which Mr. Dinwiddie seems to have been well aware from the anxiety he displayed in courting acquaintance amongst ingenious mechanics and men of experience in useful occupations, with the hopes of acquiring something new to lay before his audience. Most of the important arts and manufactures of the United Kingdom became embodied in succeeding lectures, and he was enabled to bring to his room many entirely new models of useful machinery connected with mechanics, hydrostatics, and hydraulics in particular. Among them, from Mr, Rumsey, the model of a barge to be propelled by steam becomes the subject of a lecture, a subject ordained in the course of time to effect the most astonishing revolution in the affairs of mankind. A scheme of his own for raising the Royal George received considerable approbation from his friends, but, like many other creations of the fancy, never stepped beyond the limits of theory.

As a useful and necessary adjunct to the course of lectures on modern war and naval tactics, Mr. Dinwiddie's mind was first directed, in the early part of 1790, to the science and practice of these arts among the antients. Although other arrangements required the most of his time, he entered on this new branch with much assiduity, but twelve months elapsed before he was in a condition to promulgate his researches to an audience, composed mostly of military men, including many of the gentlemen cadets at Woolwich. The following letter to the Principal of the Military Academy more fully explains the views that were entertained on this subject : —

" Sir,—On a suggestion from General Melville that a course of lectures on the science and practice of antient war, traced from the earliest times to the invention of gunpowder, might be very useful, not only to military gentlemen, but to all persons of a liberal education. I have, accordingly, for some time past, been employed in collecting materials from the antient and modern writers, together with the great light thrown on these subjects by the General. As my other avocations in business prevent me, at present, from entering on every branch of this most extensive and interesting subject, I have, by the advice of the General, and other officers of experience, begun with lectures on the subjects contained within the enclosed syllabus, as seemingly the most necessary. I take the liberty also of informing you that General Melville, having some some time ago made a communication of my intention to the Master General of the Ordnance, his Grace was pleased to give a very favourable answer in regard to the plan proposed, but to signify at the same time that no part of the time and attention of the gentlemen cadets could be spared from the necessary business of the academy, but that the antient war might be an object of private study. It is on this foundation that I presume to trouble you with the enclosed. You will please observe that, to accommodate the gentlemen cadets, the lectures are fixed for Saturday and Monday, the 29th and 31st inst.

> " I am, Sir,
> " Your most obedient servant,
"London, January 24, 1791."   " JAMES DINWIDDIE.

In the syllabus here alluded to, *the fortification and warlike engines, with the attack and defence, line of battle, and encampment, of the Greeks and Romans, are fully explained ; and models of the catapulta, balista, onager, scorpio, battering ram, &c., shown ; with the method of manufacturing the antient cordage.*

These lectures furnish the following observations on the progress of antient fortification :—

" In the first ages of society mankind wandered about in tribes, without any settled habitation. Encroachments on each other, and competitions in want became inevitable, and were soon rendered fatal. The unformed maxims of those rude ages taught them to look on every man of a different tribe as an enemy. War was the necessary consequence. Its devastations have been recorded by historians and lamented by every man of feeling; yet war has always existed, still exists, and will, in all probability, ever exist.

" To defend themselves from the hostile attacks of their neighbors, men first fixed their habitations on the tops of mountains, or rocks of difficult access. From thence they could more easily repel an invading force. The difficulty, however, of procuring subsistence for themselves and their increasing flocks soon induced them to exchange the barren mountains for the fertile plains below, and various schemes were fallen on to secure them from invasion. At length, a genius—and he possessed no mean abilities—recommended enclosing themselves and their principal effects within walls. However natural and simple this appears to us at the present day, it must have been considered by the antients as a very great invention. Of this we need no other proof than that they always ascribed the walling of their most antient cities to the gods. The walls of Troy, Thebes, and almost every very antient city, were supposed to derive their existence from a divine source. They meant, no doubt, by this to intimate that the man who either invents or improves any useful art, is the benefactor of society, and consequently resembles the gods.

"Thus, for a while, man was enabled not only to live secure within his walls, but also to extend his territories in the country. Was he likely to be attacked by a force which he could not resist in the field, he retreated within his walls, barred his gates, and set the enemy at defiance. But it was soon found that single plain walls were insufficient for protection. The defect lay here: when the enemy had carried his approaches close to the wall, he could be seen and consequently attacked only in front; on his sides and flanks he was perfectly secure. To remedy this, they built the walls with parts, at certain intervals, projecting more towards the country; and as these were exposed to the first and most vigorous attack, they behoved to be stronger, and, to give them the better command, were raised higher than the rest of the wall. Hence the introduction of towers.

"A square tower was placed with its side to the field, projecting about half its thickness beyond the wall. By this contrivance the intermediate wall, or curtain, was not only defended by its own direct fire, but also flanked by the fire of two sides of the adjoining towers. This remedy was not quite complete—one side of the tower was left to its own defence. Round towers were then substituted, from which the fire was more equally distributed. Vitruvius recommends not only the towers, but also the walls to be as nearly circular as the situation of the place would admit. Square towers, with an angle to the field, was the last and greatest improvement in antient fortification, and what gave the first hint of modern bastions.

"The attack, however, was soon found superior to the defence, and has in general continued so. No place can probably be said to be impregnable, at least by art alone. Nature and art conjointly have rendered some places, like Gibraltar, if not impregnable at least very difficult to be taken. The attack, as observed, became superior to the defence. Various tools and instruments were contrived, powerful engines were constructed, for scaling, undermining, or battering the walls. In short, when the beseigers had carried their approach up to the wall, it was found always difficult, frequently impossible to beat them off. Hence the necessity of retarding their progress by throwing every obstacle in the way. This could be done either by sinking beneath the surface of the earth some work which behoved the beseigers to fill up, or by raising another which must be beat down, before the body of the place could be reached. To effect the first purpose, a broad and deep ditch was dug all round on the outside of the walls. The form of this work is so simple as to admit of scarce any improvement, and must have been nearly as well understood by the engineer who introduced it, as it is at present, or ever will be."

"It is alleged," observes Mr. Dinwiddie in a subsequent part, "that the antients were in possession of a secret in making mortar which is now lost; and that the modern is not so durable as the antient mortar. This opinion appears to me to be unfounded. The great hardness and durability of antient mortar is chiefly owing to the mode of building. The antient walls were made so thick that the atmosphere could produce no effect on the interior parts of so great a mass of stone and mortar, which necessarily dried and consolidated in a slow and regular manner; whereas modern walls are built so thin, that the mortar dries too soon, and is consequently easily reduced to powder."

His models of the engines of war were fashioned after his own researches, and he was led into many experiments, particularly in manufacturing cordage for the balista, catapulta, &c. On this manufacture, we are told, there is not one ray of light from the antients, yet, after various attempts, he succeeded, to complete satisfaction, in spinning a number of strings of different sizes. They were formed from the tendons of animals, which, as Vigilius observes, made the only cordage that could be depended on. Another observation of this writer was confirmed, that the tendons of the hind legs of a deer are the best; those of a swine useless. The tendons were first steeped in oil, then separated into fibres, and, when half dry, spun like flax or hemp by a simple winch.

Experiments, with a sling, were made to ascertain what degree of credit attached to a belief prevalent among antient writers, who assert that leaden balls were thrown with such velocity that they became hot, and even melted in the air. It is mentioned by many antients, particularly Aristotle, who, in his treatise *De Cœlo*, speaks of it as a fact not new, but known to every one. "With such respectable testimony, Lipsius, Potter, Kennet, Adams, and every other modern writer of antiquities, rest satisfied. Indeed, it seems almost impossible to withhold assent from such convincing evidence. Must we then believe that leaden balls, thrown from a sling, were really melted by the resistance or friction of the atmosphere? No: Chemistry steps in and tells us that the alleged fact is impossible. The friction of a solid against a solid produces heat, in some cases an intense heat; but a solid against a fluid produces no heat. A musket ball receives a little heat from the inflamed powder, but a degree far short of that of melting the lead, though the velocity is much greater than that from a sling. How then are we to get over this difficulty? The antient writers had no interest, nor can we conceive they had any intention in deceiving their readers, who could easily have convicted them by an appeal to facts. We must therefore conclude that the writers were deceived themselves. The only mode of solving this difficult problem, that I can think of, is the following, which is offered not as a complete solution, but as at least extremely probable.

" I think the antients were deceived by the change of figure which a leaden ball suffers from striking a solid object, and that this change of figure might possibly exhibit appearances resembling the effects of fire in the ball. That the balls which the antient writers examined must have struck against solid bodies is evident, for they would have buried themselves in soft bodies. It therefore only remains to discover whether a hard body will produce on a leaden ball, thrown from a sling, appearances which have any resemblance to the effects of fire. For this purpose I instituted the following experiments: Balls, from the size of a musket ball to eight ounces in weight, were thrown from a sling of the proper length. The smaller balls did not exhibit any appearance to justify my conjectures ; but the result was different with balls of five or six ounces. In the latter case the ball was flattened to near one-fourth of the diameter, when the other side, particularly on the equatorial, exhibited small furrows resembling a partial fusion. This is much in favor of my explanation. A friend, with an arm much stronger than mine, threw balls from eight to twelve ounces, when the experiments succeeded to our perfect satisfaction, the resemblance of the phenomena to the effects of fire being exceedingly striking. Experiments with a musket produced a perfect imitation."

Cotemporaneous with these researches, Mr. Dinwiddie was busily engaged in extending the plan both of his public and private lectures, by very considerable additions to his apparatus. Among other improvements, the philosophical fireworks of the late Mr. Diller were added to the collection. The attraction to the lecture room by these varied and beautiful colors was great, a circumstance which proved they had the merit of being conducted by a master hand.

The month of September, 1788, was spent on a visit to the continent, particularly Paris, but for what purpose the most distant allusion can no where be traced. When harrassed by the disappointments that awaited his arrival in London, he did then anticipate introducing his lectures into the French capital. If such was his present object, either difficulties occurred or the enlargement of his views at home overbalanced the prospects of success there. Richmond-on-the-Hill appears to have been the only other place that drew him from the capital, and this happened in the summer of 1790, where he was accompanied by his apparatus, now excelling the one which terminated so unfortunately for him in Ireland. Since the commencement of his professional career, every attention had been paid to render his arrangements as effective as possible. Though not a finished orator, his introductory observations were generally very impressive. The lectures were patronised by persons of distinction, including many of the nobility: even members of the Royal Family were among those who received entertainment or instruction at his hands. But however successful his labours might be, they never seemed to raise him one step to independence.

CHAPTER III.

APPOINTMENT IN THE BRITISH EMBASSY TO CHINA—VOYAGE, AND ARRIVAL AT PEKIN.

His reputation was at its height when public attention was excited by the preparations for the Embassy to China, under the conduct of Lord Macartney. An appointment as one of the gentlemen of the suite was proffered, and at once accepted by the philosopher. The East seemed not only the field in which to extricate himself from difficulties, but to open up alluring prospects of honor as well as profit. In accomplishing the objects of the Embassy, it was meant to surprise the Chinese with the power, learning, and ingenuity of the British people, for which purpose a splendid assortment of astronomical and philosophical apparatus were among the presents to his Celestial Majesty. Included in these were a planetarium and lenses of gigantic dimensions, on the former of which the labour of thirty years had been bestowed. It was invented by, and made under the direction of, the then late P. M. Hahn, and was allowed to be the most wonderful piece of mechanism ever emanating from human hands. To do justice to this department occasioned the engagement of Mr. Dinwiddie, who was first designated *Machinest to the Embassy*, but the title not according with his feelings, that of *Astronomer* was substituted, as conveying to the mind of a

Chinese a more adequate idea of his station. In the following extract from a letter which he wrote to Lord Macartney on this subject, the duties of his province are more correctly defined to be "The erecting and regulating the planetarium; the constructing, filling, and ascending in the balloon; descending in the diving-bell; together with experiments on air, electricity, mechanics, and other branches of experimental philosophy; astronomical and other calculations." The balloon and the diving-bell were expected to be objects of great novelty and interest to the Chinese. Mr. Dinwiddie had already been to the bottom of the sea, but his ambition had never yet prompted him to an aërial voyage: he, nevertheless, looked forward with pleasure to the opportunity now offered of signalising himself by a visit to the skies on so extraordinary an occasion.

At this important juncture, another mark of distinction awaited Mr. Dinwiddie in Edinburgh, where he was promoted to the degree of *Doctor of Laws*, 13th August, 1792. Professor Dalzell, communicating this intelligence, uses the following language:—" It was with great pleasure the University conferred this mark of respect on an old alumnus, who has distinguished himself so much as you have done, particularly in natural science. I have no doubt you will continue to distinguish yourself in another quarter of the world, and contribute your share to the lustre of a mission so worthy the dignity of the British nation."

The preparations for the Embassy roused public curiosity to the highest pitch. China had long been regarded as a phenomenon among the nations of the earth. It was celebrated for its immense antiquity; for the vast number and singularity of its inhabitants, who entertained the most inflexible obstinacy in admitting strangers amongst them, and whose language, government, and daily occupations of life resembled no other portion of the human race. It was no less celebrated for beautiful scenery, and for natural productions peculiar to its own climate. To visit such a country—to have an opportunity of examining into the state of the arts and manufactures there—was a theme of overpowering interest in the mind of an ardent philosopher, and it is easy to guess the feelings with which those favored individuals, whom Government had honored on this occasion, set sail.

Besides Sir George Staunton, the Secretary of Legation, and who was also Minister Plenipotentiary, his Lordship's suite embraced twelve gentlemen holding subordinate appointments; twenty-five servants, tradesmen, mechanics and musicians; and fifty soldiers under the command of a Lieutenant-Colonel, assisted by two

lieutenants—amounting in the whole to ninety-two men.* The
Lion, man-of-war, Sir E. Gower, accompanied by the Hindostan,
East-Indiaman, was selected to convey this imposing embassy.
These vessels left Spithead, and commenced their voyage on
September 26, 1792. In discharge of duties connected with his
department, a set of chronometers were placed under the superintendence of Dr. Dinwiddie, in order to ascertain their exact
usefulness at sea, on the question of longitude. This and other
problems of nautical importance were attended to with a willingness that was ever anxious to find out the best practical applications
of science. An agreeable passage of only two months from England,
brought the ships to anchor in the harbour of Rio de Janeiro, one
of the most beautiful and spacious in the world. From a letter to
a friend in London, the following brief account is extracted:—

" During a run of upwards of six thousand miles, a great variety
of incidents, you will easily imagine, have taken place. We spent
a most agreeable week at Madeira, where we were entertained by
the Governor and English Merchants in the most superb style.
Every circumstance conspires to render this island a perfect
paradise. At Teneriffe, one of the Canaries, we spent a few days,
and exerted our utmost efforts to gain the summit of the Pico, but
the season being too far advanced, the party, after having, with
great labour, ascended to near two-thirds of the height, were obliged
to abandon the project. St. Jago, one of the Cape de Verde islands,
also received a visit, and was found in great want of provisions, no
rain having fallen for nearly two years. It is curious to remark
on the commercial relations of this place, that a Colonel of Militia
had a watch, which, for want of a key, had not gone for eight
years. We not only procured the little needful, but cleaned the
watch into the bargain. It is perhaps impossible to find a contrast

* The gentlemen and others in the suite of Lord Macartney, mentioned in
this narrative. are as follows :—

Sir George Staunton, Secretary to the Embassy.	Master Staunton (son of Sir. Geo.) Page to Lord Macartney.
Mr. Plumb, Interpreter.	Colonel Benson, Commander of the Guard.
Dr. Gillan, Physician.	Captain Parish, Assistant.
Dr. Scott, Surgeon.	Mr. H. Baring, Commissioner in the service
Mr. Maxwell, Private Secretary to Lord Macartney.	of the E. I. C.
Mr. Barrow. Controller of the Household.	Pettit Pierre, a Watchmaker.
Mr. Alexander, Draughtsman.	Victor Thibault, a Mathematical Instru-
Mr. Hickie, Portrait Painter.	ment maker.
	Eneas Anderson, servant to Lord Macartney

Anderson—(last named)—published an account of the Embassy, 1 vol., 8vo, 1795.
Staunton—published his account in 2 vols.. quarto, 1797.
Barrow—published his "Travels in China," 1 vol., quarto, 1804. 2nd edition, 1806.
Macartney—kept a Journal, published after death by Barrow, 1807.

so striking as that of the last mentioned island to our present situation. The climate of Rio de Janeiro is one of the finest on earth—the inhabitants enjoy every necessary, and most of the luxuries of life.

"Yesterday, at breakfast, I was highly amused with a relation of the disasters of the night. One gentleman had a hole, about three inches in diameter, eat by the rats through the crown of his hat. Another had his hat carried off altogether. But the attack of the mosquitoes was a matter of universal complaint, myself alone excepted. I am the only person of the suite who has enjoyed perfect good health, either of body or mind, since we left England.

"Here I first saw slavery reduced to a system. The novelty of the sight of a number of naked negro youths, at a merchant's door, attracted my attention. They were just imported from Africa, and for sale. The salesman told me, in French, he had never seen a finer cargo; held up the head of one; handled the sides of another, as a butcher does a bullock. This arose from an opinion that I wanted to be a purchaser. He was never so mistaken, nor I so shocked in all my life. The poor wretches sat on the bare ground in a state of apparent insensibility; and what affected me most of all was the affectionate concern of their predecessors in misery, several negroes of the town, endeavoring to alleviate their misfortunes by offering oranges and other fruits, which they in general refused, though their eyes, turned towards the negroes, bespoke their gratitude. In short, the various circumstances of this scene affected me more than anything I ever remember to have witnessed."

The voyage was resumed on the 17th December, in the direction of Tristan de Cunha, and the islands of Amsterdam and St. Paul, from the latter of which, after the gentlemen had made an excursion on shore, the ships were guided to the strait of Sunda, but got separated before their arrival. Approaching the strait, the Hindostan met an English vessel, which had brought to Batavia dispatches for his Lordship, accompanied by the agreeable intelligence that the Emperor had signified his intention of receiving the embassy, and that pilots were ready to conduct it through the China seas. The strait of Sunda was entered on a beautiful morning, which, with a sweet aromatic fragrance in the air, produced a most charming effect. Sumatra on the left, and Java on the right, exceedingly picturesque, rose in the distance into lofty hills, while the sea was studded with numerous isles and rocks, all covered with trees whose foliage was extremely green. At North Island, the place of rendezvous, on February 28th, the Hindostan dropped anchor to await the arrival of the Lion, which that morning hove in sight, after being lost five or six days.

The luminous appearance of an agitated sea in the dark is a curious phenomenon, which occurred under such a variety of circumstances as to baffle every hypothesis at explanation. Returning one evening from an excursion on the Sumatra side, we are told " Every stroke of the oar raised a wave of fire; even the water dripping from the oar produced a fine effect. The head of the boat was like the flames of a house on fire, and the globules, which passed along the sides, had a striking resemblance to the sparks ascending from the flames into the atmosphere." The phenomenon, which was most surprising close to the shore, gradually lessened in approaching the ship, where nothing extraordinary appeared.

From North Island the vessels, on the 4th March, sailed for the Roads of Batavia, where they anchored next day, and received the despatches. Before daylight on the 7th, a violent thunderstorm ensued, attended by heavy rain, and preceded by a most offensive smell. A flash of lightning struck the sea $1\frac{1}{2}$ miles distant, throwing up the water all round the point struck for about 50 yards, representing a vast flower pot in fireworks. It was " a grand phenomenon."

The morning of the 8th March was ushered in by the firing of cannon from the citadel, in honor of the Stadholder's birthday, and all the gentlemen of the embassy, in full uniform, were invited on shore to a sumptuous entertainment on the occasion, by the Governor. A much varied day was spent, finishing up with fireworks, and a ball which lasted to a late hour. The gentlemen, indeed, did not get to bed before two the next morning, quarters being provided for them at the hotel, " a very large and noble building." In the society of newly-acquired friends, and visiting the novelties of the place, something like a week passed before they were restored to their berths aboard ship.

Whether from unfavorable monsoons, as maintained, no attempt was made to resume the voyage for about six weeks. The scurvy meanwhile was extending on both ships, which kept frequently shifting, by short stages, from place to place. During this delay, the gentlemen were busy exploring the adjacent coasts of Sumatra and Java, as well as the numerous little islands that lay scattered around. Doctor Dinwiddie, assisted by other mathematicians, engaged in a series of trigonometrical operations, and astronomical observations, to ascertain the correct position of the principal islands and headlands by which they were surrounded, and testing the accuracy of the chart of this channel. By a very favorable observation of Jupiter's first satellite, the rate of the chronometers, too, was ascertained to a single second. For these observations two properly situated trees were generally selected, and on one occasion, as the astronomer was about to apply his eye, the head of a serpent darted from the bark, causing sufficient alarm to oblige the gentlemen to seek another station.

Towards the end of April, this tedious manœuvreing began to assume the appearance of a voyage prosecuted with vigor, in the direction of the strait of Banca. Since their entrance into the Indian seas, thunder and lightning had scarcely ceased for the space of one entire day; but no where had the latter been so intense as that which awaited their arrival off the island of Pulo Condore. "The forms were lines crossing in a great variety of beautiful figures, sometimes zig-zag, sometimes straight, with three, four, or five vibrations, almost all in horizontal directions, as from cloud to cloud. None appeared to strike the sea, and but few to dart obliquely to the highlands of the island."

Fresh provisions was the object of the visit to Pulo Condore, and, most singular to relate, after arrangements for a supply had been entered into by the natives, the party from the ships were surprised to find the houses all deserted, the inhabitants fled, and everything belonging to them left behind, with a letter on the chief's table, descriptive of their poverty and terror at the approach of such strangers. The scurvy was fearfully spread, particularly on board the Lion, which induced the commanders to crowd all sail for Turon. Approaching the bay, the Hindostan took by force an old man out of a fishing boat to pilot them into the harbor. He expected to be put to death, but through good treatment soon got the better of his fright, and spoke with a clear loud voice, but in a language quite unintelligible, even to the interpreters. Every exertion was tried to make their object understood, but to very little purpose. "It is extremely improper to give European names to places in foreign countries. When pilots are necessary, it is impossible to make them understand what you want, unless the proper name of the place is made use of." Fortune, it is said, favors the brave, and on this assistance the English had in a great measure to depend in finding the way themselves. Their first object, on casting anchor, was to erect tents and get the invalids ashore. The inhabitants were at first alarmed, but a good understanding soon prevailed; and, during a period of three weeks, the gentlemen encountered a variety of interesting adventures; among others, were entertained at a feast by the chief, or Governor of the

place.   A dramatic exhibition was got up as part of the hospitality.
"During the performance, the King's Anthem was played by Lord
Macartney's band, but the audience seemed insensible to its sublime
beauties.   Other sprightly tunes were tried with no better success.
In short, the Cochin Chinese have not the smallest taste for our
music.   Music is national, and a taste for it is probably acquired.
If Orpheus moved the oaks, it must be remembered they were
Grecian oaks, and Orpheus a Greek musician."

In four days from resuming the voyage, the Ladrone islands were
seen to bear on every point of the compass.   Here another but
short respite ensued, while Sir G. Staunton went to Macao on
business connected with the Embassy, taking with him two Chinese
missionaries, and returning with two others, "one of whom, P.
Hanna, an Irishman, is mentioned by La-Lande as having set out
for China in 1788, to continue the astronomical observations.
He has been at Macao ever since, (five years), having never,
during that time been able to procure a passage, or mode of
conveyance to Pekin."

When Sir George returned, the ships set sail for Chusan, off which
the anchor was again let go, in order to procure pilots to conduct
them to the Peiho river.   Hitherto the voyage had presented much
agreeable novelty, but here it began to assume a more than usual
interest.   In sight, at one time, were counted no fewer than two
hundred fishing boats, each boat with ten or twelve men, many of
whom came on board expressing great surprise at the bulk of the
ship, the height of the masts, &c.   They were strong in appearance, and well shaped, with a slight tinge of sable in their complexion ; extremely good natured, and showing a great degree of
curiosity, which was looked upon as a good omen.   An old pilot
entered into arrangements to go ashore and purchase some buffaloes
and other articles for the ship.   He was furnished with the money,
and left his companions as hostages.   The next day he arrived with
four bullocks, which cost only fifty-two dollars.   All kinds of provisions were remarkably cheap ; two hundred eggs cost but a dollar
and a half.

When the Hindostan had been at anchor a few days, a mandarin
of high rank, with several attendants, came aboard in his official
capacity.   "His dress was a pale yellow, with a blue glass globe
in his little white conical hat, or bonnet.   His boots were of black
silk with thick soles, broad at the toes and no heels.   No buttons of
any sort were seen in any of their dresses.   He was very polite,
appeared quick and skilled in his business, and wrote fast.   His
face very much resembled that of Henry the Eighth.   He asked a

number of questions, took down the names of the ship, Lord Macartney, and Captain McIntosh; whither going, the presents, the number of guns, length and breadth of the ship, &c. During these proceedings dinner was preparing in his own boat, and, when ready, it was put into baskets and brought aboard the Hindostan, in the balcony of which he dined. He was a good hearty fellow, and dexterously handled his two chop-sticks in lifting the fish, &c., which composed the dinner. Sauce was a necessary accompaniment, and lifted by a spoon about the size of a large tablespoon. I tasted every dish, and found them extremely good and well flavored. Samsu, a spirituous liquor, is perfectly clear, and tastes exactly like good whiskey. When standing on the deck one of his attendants scratched his back."

Several other mandarines came on board through motives of curiosity. " All of them had pipes, which were lighted with a little bit of fungus, or touch-wood, kindled by a spark from a flint and steel. The attendant who lights the pipe, takes a whiff or two himself, then gives it to the mandarine, after wiping it with his hand. The pipe was a little metal bole, with a smooth black shank. These mandarines drank several cups of samsu. The cup resembles a tea-cup, but deeper in proportion, and holds about a common glass-full."

Sir George Staunton, and the party who went ashore respecting the pilots, found much difficulty in settling the question. They sat, it seems, for three hours in the house of the chief mandarine, who asked a thousand questions; but the secretary would neither taste nor drink till the pilots were procured. A mandarine of letters produced the edict of the Emperor, who wanted the Embassy to be conducted from province to province.

The prosecution of the voyage seems now to have demanded more than usual attention, as was made manifest by every exertion to get forward. On every side the course from Chusan was beset with shallows and rocky isles, and rendered still more dangerous from remarkably thick fogs, that ensued for several successive evenings. The frequent and sometimes long delays had been a great drawback on the Embassy; they were now, however, steering along the coast of the country so much the object of their desires, and towards which every eye was turned with the most lively feelings of curiosity. Though at times barren, at other times the land was under cultivation, and quite pleasing. In many places, on the sides of the hills, the ground was reduced to a level, by terraces carried parallel to the horizon, a mode of farming peculiar to the Chinese. The prospect embraced villages, detached houses, trees, fields, and people at work, sometimes collected into groups on rising ground, gazing at the strange ships as they moved past. Innumerable islands, and many curiously figured rocks, not unlike the work of art, were constantly bringing a change of view; while fishing boats, in every direction, continued to ply their vocations—all drawing largely on the attention of the visitors to this interesting portion of the globe.

The voyage terminated on the 30th July, and finished the Doctor's calculations for the longitude. "This last sight concludes my observations in the Hindostan, where I have assisted at the taking, and calculated every sight in both chronometers and lunar observations during the voyage of ten months. Upon the whole, I am of opinion, that though chronometers be extremely useful at sea, and that no captain should be without two at least, yet, in long voyages, the main dependence must ever be on the lunar observation. Experience also convinces me, that when the lunar sights are taken at proper times; when the distance is carefully observed, and the calculations properly made, the error, arising from a series of three sets of observations, will seldom exceed five miles from the truth. I would never take a single sight when the altitude was less than ten degrees, but if above thirty so much the better."

Arrangements for forwarding the Embassy being completed, on the morning of the 5th August, Lord Macartney and his suite left the ships for the Peiho river, under a salute of fifteen guns, and the most hearty cheers of those who remained behind. His Lordship and some of the gentlemen were carried ashore in the brigs attending the Embassy; the rest of the retinue got aboard a number of junks provided on the part of the Chinese. "The junks are all built alike, considerably raised at the head and stern, with an elevated superstructure between on deck. The head and stern rise by gradual curves, not by steps, the curves of both being nearly alike. The junk itself is perfectly flat-bottomed, and nearly of the same width throughout. Each has two masts, with sails of matting or canvass, all of a rectangular form, and hoisted by ropes going over tails at the mast-head. Blocks are straight and flat without strapping, the rope being passed through a hole below the sheave, an inferior plan to strapping. Cables consist of four strands, each of which is again formed from a number of smaller strands, much twisted, without the appearance of any substance similar to tar or pitch. The anchor is of iron, and consists of four round flukes, about two and a half feet long, making an angle of seventy degrees with the shank, which is octagonal. It has no stock, but is provided with a ring and a screw at the end. There is also a ring at

the further end.   The rudder is placed between two cheeks at the
stern.   It is very broad, the upright part round, and rises seven or
eight feet above the deck.   A high tiller, of the usual length, is
fixed too near the upper end, and strengthened by two side pieces
bound together by a strong iron strap.   Two ropes from the sides
make nearly a right angle at the tiller.   The cabin is raised three
feet above the level of the deck, and consists of a slender frame of
split bamboos covered with mats, about nine feet by six on the
plan, and not more than four feet in height.   The galley is fitted
with stoves, and the conveniences for cooking excellent.   We dined
at noon, on a leg of mutton cooked with rice, sitting cross-legged
upon the floor, without either chair, table, cloth, knife, fork, or
spoon, and we had not sufficiently practised the chopsticks to be
able to make any use of them."

Approaching the mouth of the river, the coast was of a beautiful
green from the extensive appearance of a plant extremely useful in
China for fuel, matting, and a variety of other purposes.   In their
way up the river the junks beat against both wind and tide, but
eventually had to be towed by some of the men on shore, great
numbers having been drawn to the place by so unusual an event.
One end of the rope is fastened to the mast-head, the other end to
both ends of a stick laid over the right shoulder of a man, the rope
in front, and coming below the left arm.   Those behind the foremost pull by offsets.   The flow of the tide was regular but very
rapid, and, at high water, about as broad as the Thames.   All along
the crowd was great, composed of women as well as men.   Towards
evening the fleet came to rest at the village of Ta-coo, where the
shore presented a long line of military, decorated with eighteeen
stand of colours.   Here the head mandarine had enlarged his house,
by the addition of two large pavilions, to receive the Ambassador
and his suite.   His Lordship, Sir George, and the Interpreter, accepted the invitation, but the gentlemen remained for the night on
board the junks, although the accommodations were in no way
inviting.   There was not room for five cots in the cabin, and lying
on the bare boards, covered by a single mat, proved so very disagreeable, that the Doctor changed his situation for the open deck, where
he slept in the coil of the cable for half the night.

The boats which were to carry them up the river lay ready here,
and the next morning the whole suite moved into them, finding
accommodations much superior to those they had just left.   That
appointed for our informant and four other gentlemen had six apartments, the two aftermost being used as kitchens, and another for
their dining room, where also two cots were fixed.   The cot rested

D 2

upon a platform raised twenty-two inches above the floor. The doors were heavy and badly varnished, and turned upon two hinges, consisting of wooden pins fixed to the inside of the door, and fitting into round holes in pieces of wood in the lintel and threshold. Windows of oyster shells, with panes about one inch and a quarter square, wrought upon hinges similar to the doors. Sometimes in the middle a piece of silk flowed in a pretty manner, and very transparent.

Every arrangement for the prosecution of the journey was completed on the evening of the eighth, when the British band played up for the first time, seemingly with as little impression on the Celestial seamen as upon the Cochin-Chinese at Turon. At noon, the next day, the famous passage up the Peiho commenced, and, in regular succession, the boats moved forward by human labor, the men exerting themselves like horses. Curiosity had reached its highest pitch, and the weather, smiling on the travellers, was serene but very hot—the thermometer ranging from ninety to ninety-six degrees. Impressions of an agreeable nature marked the early part of their journey. "The curvilineal meanderings of the river are most enchanting. In the space of a few hours we sail upon every point of the compass; the river still maintains its breadth, and the country, although level, is enriched with villas, trees, and cultivated fields."

At noon, on the 10th August, an altitude of the sun was observed by a sextant, the operation being watched with great interest by the Chinese on board. The altitude was taken through mere curiosity, and brought out the latitude 39° 10'. "Probably," as remarked, "the first observation of the kind on this river; at any rate, the first with an English sextant and by a Briton."

Shortly after the boats approached the side of the river, and, for the first time, the Doctor set foot on Chinese ground, which had been in sight for seven or eight weeks; but he was soon obliged to return on board from the great curiosity of the people, who came flocking about him. The plant of a dye stuff was here extensively cultivated. On the Doctor picking up a sprig of it, a fellow presented him with a prickly vegetable, of no value, to occasion a laugh. Some of the lower people were apt to take such liberties if indulged in, but were easily checked, and on the whole they behaved with much civility.

On the banks of the river, large stacks of salt had frequently arrested the attention, but approaching Tiensin, the whole Embassy was struck with astonishment at the immense quantities of this important article that were brought to view. The salt was contained in baskets, and built into heaps, somewhat resembling military tents, but much larger. Where the river divides into two branches, a bridge of boats was seen to stretch across. In a moment the bridge disappeared, and on passing the place where it stood, the boats were found arranged on either side. In ten minutes after, the Embassy reached the large and populous city of Tiensin. The number of spectators collected here was prodigious. Every inch on shore, and on the decks of at least five hundred ships, was crowded to excess, all eager to gratify curiosity at the sight of the illustrious strangers.

A communication, previously received from His Excellency, acquainted such gentlemen as wished to accompany him ashore to be ready, in full dress, so soon as the boats came to rest. They were to meet an Envoy from the Emperor, the Governor of the province, and other mandarines of distinction; and accordingly the whole suite was conducted, with much parade, to a pavilion erected on purpose. To keep the crowd at a distance, the officers whipped them most un-mercifully. His Lordship occupied the left, and the Governor the right of the room, while the gentlemen were seated on two rows of chairs, opposite and parallel to those on which the mandarines sat. Lord Macartney, Sir George, and the Interpreter, were on an elevated kind of table, or bench; all the others on a level. The chairs were of the usual height, with cushions on bamboo bottoms, and a piece of red satin doubled over the back. Each mandarine had a small footstool, as it is fashionable in China to sit with the bottom on a level with the heels. The pavilion was covered and lined with mats painted on the inside, and supported by pillars, apparently of bamboo, wrapt round with red silk. A matting, and over that a kind of thin silk gauze, covered the floor.

The ceremony, which was neither interesting nor the object of it very apparent, lasted only about twenty minutes, when the gentle-men took their leave to return on board, followed by a most sump-tuous dinner from the Governor. Some of the junks had enough for three times the number intended.

A row of fine looking houses fronted the beach, and full in the view of the boats, a theatre, having the appearance of elegance, was attended by a crowded audience of seemingly genteel company; but our informant sets down as "insipid stuff" the performance, which had commenced before their arrival, and continued without intermission till they were again out of sight.

Exactly at one, after a respite of three hours, the Embassy moved forwards, passing a large body of military with a most unmilitary looking appearance. Their dress was blue, with a heavy iron helmet tied beneath the chin—the crest, a long spike projecting obliquely backwards, by which "the soldier might be

easily strangled." Some were armed with Tartar bows, one end
placed in a leathern case, the other projecting towards the front,
with the string undermost. The arrows, in a quiver, hung behind
the shoulder. Both the bow and arrow were similar to specimens
employed in the lecture room in London, on the subject of antient
war. A sabre hung on the left side, with the point projecting to
the front. Others shouldered most miserable looking matchlocks.
Every twenty-four, or so, had a stand of tawdry colors, besides
lesser colors between every two or three men.

Some miles beyond Tiensin, where the river again divided into
two branches, the Embassy stopped to receive the visit from the
Envoy, who came attended by a great procession, conspicious with
officers, colors, gongs, &c. Here two tents were erected, and a row
of beautiful red lanterns placed along the whole range of the ships,
which came to rest for the night.

The mandarines in charge of the Embassy conducted everything
with great regularity. A plentiful supply of provisions, consisting
of mutton, pork, fowls, and other animal food, with a number of
Chinese compound dishes, tea, eggs, &c., were daily in readiness.
There were also a great variety of fruits, such as apples, peaches,
cucumbers, water melons, and sometimes grapes. Samsu and even
ice water were always at command. Presents, in brown paper
parcels, were occasionally distributed among the gentlemen. On
the parcels were pasted strips of red paper, containing the names
of the articles written in Chinese. "The vast attention paid us by
all ranks is extremely flattering." One of the conducting mandarines is described as a hearty fellow, seemingly enjoying the task
committed to his charge. His yacht was at the head of the procession ; and after inviting the Doctor and his messmates to tea with
him there, he returned with the gentlemen in the happiest humour
imaginable. He both danced and sung, imitating with his voice a
few tunes played on the flute by Mr. Hickie, and which he also
accompanied by striking some tea-cups and basons on the table
with his fan. The different folds of the fan exhibited different
figures. On his left wrist he wore a hoop of gold wire more than
a quarter inch in thickness, and sufficiently large to go over his
hand. The ends were brought together, but not united, like a ring
for keys. He pronounced English words with great readiness,
such as *Very well, How do you do ;* but laboured in vain at *broth.*

"Lord Anson remarks that the Chinese had so little curiosity as
hardly to look at his ship, though they had never seen anything
like it. The Abbe Raynal observes on this remark, that the
Chinese were too much occupied to satisfy our idle curiosity—they

were better employed. We have found matters very different, for every little village we pass pours out an incredible number of inhabitants, all most eagerly curious to see us, and seem to be perfectly idle, for they attend us sometimes two hours or more, sitting at their ease on the banks of the river, and on the decks of such vessels as happen to be near. They even wade into the river, and up to the neck; and many of them will swim to the vessel to get a nearer prospect of us."

The Chinese peasants were, nevertheless, accustomed to the hardest work, which they underwent without murmuring. " In perpetually tracking against the current of a strong stream, without the least aid from the wind, the men were sometimes up to the middle in mud and water; at other times obliged to swim across rivulets entering the Peiho; all this with great cheerfulness; nor does it seem to proceed so much from the commands of the mandarine, as from a natural willingness to do their duty. The men who transhipped our luggage, under a most excessively hot sun, never asked either money or drink, though they do not dislike samsu, even sometimes get tipsy with it. Their dexterity in hoisting up, and still more in carrying the heaviest boxes, appeared to me far superior to anything I had ever seen in Europe."

Some of the Chinese on board the junks practised the art of dissimulation in keeping back part of the provisions, which however were always given up with a good grace. " When the captain is desired to enumerate the articles sent by the mandarines, he never fails to mention the article secreted, and says, it is in such a place. It is immediately brought. A very barefaced trick was attempted by the cook serving two fowls, each without a leg. When signified that a fowl had two legs, he laughingly pointed to the dish into which they had been put. This servant was promised a cup of samsu one evening, and the next morning made signs for it. When desired to remove the cover from the jar and serve himself, he added the liberty of carrying it to the kitchen, but returned in a minute or two, having taken out a quart at least, and offering his bowl with a smile for the promised liquor."

Vessels were continually in sight descending the river by the current alone, gliding with the stern foremost at an angle of about forty-five degrees, occasioned by the particular position of the rudder. Several families, it appeared, lived on board of each. "A junk draws so little water, on account of being perfectly flat, that it not only goes up the shallow rivers and canals, but a dock, for repairing any damage, can be made in a few hours on the side of the river, where several docks, with sometimes boats in them,

were seen.   In shallow water the rudder is raised by a rope, which
extends underneath, and goes round the windlass.   The windlass is
of the usual form, without pauls, their place being supplied by
handspikes.   Depths are sounded by a long taper bamboo, having
two or three circles of hair tied round it with rope yarn.   On the
return of the tide, the ship's head is apt to get too far from the
shore, and to prevent this, two of the towers, considerably behind,
are provided with a small wooden anchor with one fluke, which they
thrust into the ground.   This gives the ship's head a tug towards
the bank, but the anchor must be pulled out immediately.   The
shank and fluke are fastened by iron straps, and the fluke pointed in
iron.   The shanks of all their anchors are octagonal; and boat
hooks, oars, &c., have all a cross piece in the handle, like a spade,
which seems useful.   When pulling, the sailors sing out, and alter
their voices towards the conclusion.   When sculling at the great
oar, which rests on a pivot projecting from the side of the vessel
near the head, they use a tune almost the same as the "Highland
Laddie."   The sails on horizontal bamboos have one advantage over
the European—they have no belly.   The necessary is very inconvenient, exposing the greater part of the body.   In ship-building, the
Chinese use a kind of cement that renders the vessel always tight;
certain it is that a pump has not yet been seen in any even of their
largest ships.   This cement is composed of lime made from oyster
shells, mixed with oil and a little bamboo scrapings, which latter
answers the purpose that hair does in English plaster.   Hanging at
the head door of every vessel is a gong, which is beat as a signal for
making or slacking sail.   They seem all of the same dimensions,
about 2½ to 3 feet diameter.   In the centre is a cavity, or hollow
part, convex on the inside, about seven inches across and one inch
deep.   Though harsh and disagreeable when beat, nevertheless, the
handle, dangling downwards, gently touched by the wind, occasionally
produced an Æolian concert of astonishingly sweet chords."

   Nothing conspired to break the monotonous level of the country
till towards the evening of the 14th, when, for the first time, the
high hills of Tartary, far in the distance, became visible, and presented something like a termination to their long voyage.   The river
at this juncture was become extremely shallow, and a considerable
drawback on the progress of the boats.   As usual, the banks presented crowds of spectators, with the upper part of the body generally
uncovered, and exposing the skin tanned by the heat of a burning
summer sun.   Black hair and white teeth were universally charac-
teristics.   Tobacco was occasionally indulged in, but none appeared
to chew betel, as reported by some writers on China.   Women were

frequently in the crowd, but generally behind the men, and seldom approached the banks. "All parties seem much diverted at our dress, particularly the breeches, so different from their loose garments."

An object which could not fail to be matter of surprise was the constant display of the military, posted in large bodies, frequently at short intervals, either on the right or left bank of the river. Their dress occasionally varied; but always unsoldierlike, and their march tumultuous. Bows, sabres, and matchlocks, were the only distinguishable weapons, nor had a single firelock been seen on the journey. At one place a salute of three rounds was fired from a piece which could not be distinctly perceived, but appeared to be a kind of firework. Every military station had tents conspicuous for size and show.

Confined as the travellers were to the boats, between which but little intercourse could happen, their sources of information rested entirely on their eyes, assisted by the exertions of imagination. Nothing observable of much scientific knowledge transpired; and not one single structure of any kind, remarkable for size or grandeur, could be seen. Houses, everywhere, were of one story, and, from their peculiar appearance, the walls were at first considered to be formed of mud, but were afterwards found to be built of brick, said to be dried in the sun. Bricks seemed to be the chief material used in building. Roofs, covered with tiles of a similar nature, were nearly at the same angle of fashionable houses in Europe. Several of those square brick towers, mentioned by all writers on China, drew the attention of the English travellers. Part of a curious monumental tower bore some resemblance to a kind of dome, from the centre of which rose a spire with a number of belts, or circular bandages, seemingly cut out of the wood or stone, of which the whole is composed. Little or no masonry had been distinguished beyond a few stone bridges of one arch, but more approaching the parabolic form. The voussoirs were extremely large and irregular, and the key-stone, particularly one, very small. All of them were in bad repair. Some wooden bridges, seen at a distance, exhibited nothing remarkable. A week's sail up the Peiho had transpired when the first two-wheeled carriage was noticed in the country. It was covered like a common waggon, and altogether clumsy in appearance. An object of peculiar novelty was seen in a man wheeling a barrow with a sail.

Tonshu, another large city, terminated the journey by water. Their arrival was late in the afternoon, but the gentlemen did not leave the boats till the next morning, when a public breakfast was prepared for them in a spacious temple of Fo. Immediately afterwards the transhipping of the luggage required every attention at the river. After a day of great fatigue, the whole sixteen junks were unloaded, and every article safely lodged in two long sheds erected for the purpose. These sheds were respectively two hundred and fifty-seven feet in length, and one hundred and twenty-four in breadth; but the whole of this space was not covered over. For several days all was attention at the sheds, where the presents and other baggage were arranged in two divisions, preparatory to being sent forward to Pekin—the one to be carried on waggons, and the other on men's shoulders. The mode of fitting up the latter by long bamboo poles was simple, but obvious.

The temple was converted into lodgings for the Embassy during its temporary residence at Tonshu. Eight gentlemen were to have slept in one apartment, but such was the heat that two of them preferred the portico, and in consequence of the appearence of a scorpion another gentleman followed.

This sacred edifice consists of a number of chapels and other apartments. The columns have no pedestal, and are nearly equally thick throughout, terminated at the upper end by a large semicircular frieze, without any capital. In the portico colonnade, the row of outside pillars is made fast to those in the building by cross pieces, whose rectangular tenons pass through the pillar, near the upper end of the shaft, with sometimes a pin driven through the projecting part of the tenon lengthwise, in the form of a wedge, to keep all fast. The area is paved with bricks ten inches long and five by two and a half in breadth and thickness; and the roof is covered with semicircular tiles, the convex side downwards. An almost cylindrical tile, running up and down, covers the joinings. The windows are of paper and thin silk. Some of the silk gauze is so thin that at a distance it becomes invisible, and looks like very transparent glass. A number of lamps, made of silk, with flowers of colored paper, very neatly executed, constantly burns before the shrine. Some of them are square; others hexagon, the first instance of this figure coming under notice—the octagon being by far the most common. The bell has eight scollips, with five holes in the crown, placed in two lines crossing at right angles, which the Chinese say increases the tone. It has no clapper, being struck by a billet of soft thready wood. The gongs on board the boats are struck by a similar instrument, not covered with netting, like some seen from Canton. A large picture, in the temple, exhibits the most complete ignorance of a knowledge of the art of painting. People at a distance figure taller than a house at hand, and do not seem to touch the ground. Every object is drawn without the shadow.

An eclipse of the moon, which was about to take place, seems to have been an object of some interest to the Chinese. " I have received from our conductor, Vantagin, an account of the eclipse which happens to-morrow, (21st August), in Chinese, but our interpreter cannot translate it. I wish much to compare it with the calculations I have made out, and with the type I handed to Lord Macartney yesterday."

During their stay at Tonshu, a trial was made of two six pounders, which formed part of the presents to the Emperor. They fired about seven rounds in a minute, but the mandarines did not seem much pleased with the performance, and intimated they could fire as quick at Pekin. "The following circumstance, perhaps, contributed to form the opinion of some of them. Just before the firing began, some men were passing on the opposite side of the river, at least six hundred yards distant. Several of the mandarines observing them, immediately ran towards the side of the river, hollowing, and making all the most significant signs for them to get out of the way; but afterwards finding Mr. Parish stand during the firing within twelve or fifteen yards of the muzzle of the pieces, contempt was the consequence. The more ignorant men are, the more are they offended at the discovery of their ignorance."

Wednesday, the 21st August, was appointed for resuming the journey towards Pekin, which was now but twelve miles distant. As their cots had been sent forward the preceding evening, the gentlemen had to pass the night on stools, tables, benches, &c., and of course rose not over refreshed for the journey, to which they were summoned by the sound of a drum as early as two o'clock. At four the procession began, passing direct through the city of Tonshu, which was large, and surrounded by thick walls, at least twenty-five feet in height. His Lordship, Sir G. Staunton, and the Interpreter, occupied sedan chairs, and, with one other exception on horseback, the gentlemen all chose to ride in two-wheeled carriages, which had neither springs nor seat, and the only alternative was to sit on the bottom, cross-legged, the usual manner of the Chinese, or lean over the side at the bottom of one of the shafts. The bottom was carpeted with a piece of cloth, and overhead was a covering like a common waggon. Some of the carriages were drawn by one, others by two horses, with wooden saddles—the second horse having both its traces hooked to the same point at the bottom of the shaft. The wheels had eighteen spokes, and rather narrow rims, but very deep and strong. No order of travelling had been settled, and the procession was not remarkable for regularity, as parties took the liberty of getting before one another. Great crowds were early collected, and, as the morning advanced, the heat of the sun became excessive. What little could be seen of the country was very indifferent, and nothing stylish whatever indicated the approach to the capital of the " flowery kingdom." Breakfast was prepared at a village on the way, about seven o'clock, and at half-past nine, after passing through an extensive suburb, the travellers entered the great gate of Pekin, the fondest object of their aspirations; but, notwithstanding the wonderful features it presented, it fell short of the pictures which imagination had conjured up. Before them extended a wide street, crowded with spectators, and bounded by irregular built houses, mostly of one story, with here and there some edifices distinguished for grandeur and extent. A short delay ensued at the entrance, where refreshments were provided, and the cavalcade moving forwards, at noon passed through the opposite gate. Six miles beyond this gate, near the village of Hatien, stood the mansion appointed to lodge the Embassy, which reached its destination exactly at two o'clock. On alighting, the gentlemen were kept standing in a passage, in the most tiresome suspense, before they were permitted to follow the Ambassador, or know what to do, and experiencing the greatest inconvenience from the want of an interpreter. Unable from fatigue to stand it longer, they all marched in a body in quest of his Lordship and Mr. Plumb, whom they found disputing with the mandarines about the apartments not being sufficiently spacious. However, this they had to submit to for the present, and after drinking a couple of dishes of tea, the Doctor went to bed, being much indisposed with his bones almost dislocated from the jolting of the *car.* He, however, rose again at eight to attend to the eclipse, and found the Chinese honoring the event with the noise of bells, drums, gongs, &c., " ceremonies which none but the ignorant observe."* After the lapse of eleven months, the Embassy, at least for our informant, had thus arrived at the journey's end.

* This eclipse is mentioned by Barrow as having occurred while at Tonshu, causing there a day of rest to the Embassy, which is contrary to the fact, even to Barrow himself. Lest some reader who has seen the " Travels in China " should be surprised to find the two narratives clash in this manner, it has been deemed advisable to state that the stories related by Barrow are, as a whole, pure inventions to support whims and prejudices; and in consequence a few of them are noticed here to put the reader on his guard. A detailed investigation of the " Travels in China " has already appeared in another work.

CHAPTER IV.

RESIDENCE AT PEKIN.

IN the vicinity of Hatien lay the Imperial palace of Yuen-min-yuen, which was appointed for the reception of the presents, and where the astronomical and philosophical portion were to be fixed and properly adjusted. Thither Dr. Dinwiddie accompanied Lord Macartney and Sir George Staunton to examine the apartments, and deliberate on the best mode of arrangement. In the great hall, containing the Emperor's throne, they met a high mandarine and two missionary interpreters. The east end of the hall was selected for the planetarium, while the globes had their portion, one on each side of the throne. Appropriate situations were also fixed upon for the orrery, Vulliamy's clocks, lustres, &c. While viewing the great hall the party were not a little surprised to find a musical clock which played " Catherine Ogie," and a number of other tunes, and having the name of Clarke, Leadenhall-street, on the dial plate.

In this edifice, where never European slept before, Dr. Dinwiddie, Mr. Barrow, and the two mechanics, took up their residence to adjust the presents* previous to the arrival of the Emperor, who was then in Tartary. In the mean time, the Ambassador and the rest of the suite removed from Hatien to more spacious apartments in Pekin, from which they set out, September 2nd, to meet his Celestial Majesty at Zehol, in Tartary.

When the Embassy first reached the capital it was deeply regretted that there was only one interpreter, who was too much occupied at head quarters to be of any service to gentlemen in other places. So great was the inconvenience, even to the Chinese, that the Emperor called in some Portuguese missionaries to supply the desideratum. Previous, however, to the arrival of these missionaries the heads of the Embassy, from some preconceived aversion, issued orders to hold no conversation whatever. Latin being the only medium of discourse, was strictly forbidden to be spoken at all.† The gentlemen were much at a loss to know the reason of this prohibition, and the consequence was, some scenes bordering on the ridiculous took place. One father addressed Dr. Gillan: *Tu loquaris Latinum, Domine? Mum!* "Learned Doctors not speak Latin!" exclaims the philosopher with surprise,

---

* Besides the scientific instruments, there were many other presents, consisting of the finest specimens of English art and manufacture. These were placed under the care of Barrow.

† This prohibition to speak *Latin* is totally ignored by Barrow, no doubt in deference to his patron Sir George Staunton, who issued the order.

startled at the ideas which would naturally arise in the minds
of the Portuguese. It was too well known that most men of reputation in science, as well as literature, throughout every country in
Europe, cultivated an acquaintance with the Latin language, in
which most of the learned works were originally written; and to try
to impress the Portuguese fathers with the idea that the gentlemen
of the Embassy could not speak it, was not only lowering their
dignity, but asserting what evidently was not true. Sir George
Staunton, though speaking Latin himself to the Interpreter, in the
hearing of the missionaries, sent a letter to the palace forbidding the
Doctor to make use of it to the Portuguese, or an Italian, named
Diodati, also called in for the same purpose. The letter was
received through the hands of Diodati, who presented it with a
significant glance at the motto on the seal—*Fiat Responsio.*
Silence under the circumstances might be a master stroke of policy,
but the artifice was too shallow to escape the penetration of the
missionaries, whose respect for the English was no way enhanced.
But to show what ridiculous shuffling was adopted, Father Diodati
was, after all, allowed to become the interpreter at the palace, and
to converse with the gentlemen in a language which, a few days
before, they (the gentlemen) could not understand.

The arrival of the presents created a deal of curiosity, and among
the visitors were many mandarines, who seemed pleased with the
appearance of the instruments, but showed how little they were
acquainted with the sciences. One asked: "*Where are the five
planets on the celestial globe?* All are surprised to find China so
small on the terrestrial; and some fancy it is made small by the
Hungmee (English) on purpose. The Chinese act very much like
children: are as easily pleased and as soon tired." The operations
were daily interrupted by three youths, grandsons of the Emperor.
One of them had a capped and jewelled watch (by Cummin, of
London), which was much in want of cleaning, and it was put
through the hands of a workman, who brought it into a state of
activity it seems not to have enjoyed for some time. Another of
the princes once observed to a missionary: "*The English must be
very proud of their knowledge in science, when they make such a
parade in bringing so many fine machines to China.*"

The three Portuguese, to whom no one could speak Latin, belonged
to the Tribunal of Mathematics, and arrived with orders to see the
presents, and have everything explained. Among them, Father
Andreas was one of the presidents—the other president being a
Tartar. These missionaries had the calculations to make every
year for the almanac. The Emperor himself was extremely anxious

to know the nature and merits of the various instruments, and Diodati had instructions to carry an accurate description, particularly of the orrery, to compare it with an instrument at the palace in Tartary. Before setting out, this father had the benefit of a lecture on the use and structure of the machine particularised by his Majesty.*

The erection and regulation of the planetarium was the grand object to be effected. It was first of all put temporarily together, and completed in appearance, when Mr. Alexander came to take a perspective representation of it to accompany Lord Macartney into Tartary; eighteen days, however, elapsed before the machine was thoroughly cleaned, fixed in its place, and adjusted to its proper motion. "It has been a troublesome job, not owing to any difficulty in the work, but the inconvenience arising from a number of impertinent eunuchs, keepers of the palace, who made so much noise, and what they thought fun, that it was frequently impossible to attend to the business. The planetarium will by this mode of erecting lose much of its effect. An ignorant people should always be taken by surprise. When a grand machine is shown all at once, and the principles of motion concealed, it seldom fails in its effect. But when it is shown piecemeal; when the various detached parts are exhibited and put together in their sight—in short, when the machine is built from its foundation before them, the time seems long; they impute every trifling mistake or hesitation in the workman about placing this or that part, which can be known most frequently only by trial, to a want of knowledge in the machine, and want of ability in the profession. For example, when the platform was laying, and it became necessary to select such pieces as belonged to such and such parts, which, together with making the whole fast and level, took up a good deal of time, the men were told they labored much and did nothing. From all which I am of opinion that the machine is much lowered in the estimation of the people about the palace, and that the prejudices entertained by the Chinese respecting the ingenuity and address of our workmen will

* One of the most impudent anecdotes related by Barrow is, that of the "Emperor's Favorite Draughtsman." The Emperor, we are told, sent such a personage to the palace to take views of the scientific machines, and bring them with descriptions to his Majesty in Tartary. Now Mr. Dinwiddie, who had the control of these machines—who resided constantly at the palace —and who duly records all visitors and others waiting upon him—is entirely ignorant of the existence of the "Favorite Draughtsman." But curiously, he tells us that Mr. Alexander, Draughtsman to the Embassy, did draw some of the machines, which drawings, with descriptions, were taken by the missionary, Diodati, to the Emperor. All this is evidently the foundation on which Barrow tries to build up a whim prejudicial to Chinese artists.

be confirmed. I gave it as my opinion, long before our arrival in China, that not only the planetarium, but all the other presents, should be properly fitted up before they were seen at all, even by the mandarines, if possible, and experience has now convinced me of the propriety of that opinion."

At the expiration of three weeks, and before the Ambassador's return from Tartary, the party removed from the palace, where the lodgings were damp, to those provided in the city; but the Doctor returned almost daily to inspect the movements of the planetarium, his chief care. The palace was some eight or nine miles distant from the hotel in the city, and these visits were accomplished in a Chinese carriage, under the guidance of a mandarine, who was remarkably punctual in driving the Doctor to and from his duties; in fact, with all the regularity of a mail coach. As formerly observed, these carriages were without springs, and upon two wheels; and it is singular that, amongst the great many constantly coming in view, not one of any description with four wheels could be seen. Great carts or waggons have sometimes wheels with spokes like the carriages, but more generally made with one large cross, crossed by two smaller ones. The paving stones of the road, when laid down, were observed to be fluted a little lengthwise, an improvement by which the horse never misses foot.

Between Pekin and the palace the drive was never varied, except in two instances, when the capital only was entered at a different gate. "That part of the wall which we daily pass is extremely well built, with square towers at seemingly equal intervals, each interval containing about thirty embrasures, calculated for bows and arrows, or matchlocks, rather than cannon. Guns of this description are nowhere to be seen, and where kept can as little be conceived. Every second merlon has a round hole a little below the level of the embrasure, which is a rectangular opening, generally about one-fourth of the merlon. Each tower has five or six embrasures in front and in flank, placed in a line with the battlements of the curtain. The slope of the flanks is considerable; and the thickness of the parapet equals the length of one brick. The walls are formed of earth, cased in bricks, fifteen or sixteen inches long, about one-half in breadth, and one-fourth in thickness. The arches of the gates are composed of three arches within each other, with the bricks placed endwise towards the centre. Judging from the gates, the walls must be about twenty feet thick, all in an antient style; yet the brick does not seem old, and I am of opinion that the walls are not so old as is alleged."

Some details of Chinese architecture mention that "the roofs of he temple and other well-built houses are curved, convexity downwards, projecting about one-fourth of the columns like the Tuscan in Covent Garden. Columns have no capital. Two pieces of wood join the upper part of the column with the wall, and are seen within the portico : the uppermost projects on the inside of the wall and bears the joists, which do not rest on the wall. Doors consist of two rectangular frames divided into three, four, or more panels, and have generally inscriptions on them. They are barred with two flat pieces, which are fixed alternately on the half door, one above, the other below, so as to divide the door in height into three parts. These pass through and into the opposite side. Door frames are the same below as above; hence, on entering every door and gate at the palace, one has to step over a cross piece of wood from six to twelve inches deep. Locks, small and great, are of the same construction, and in general may be easily opened with a stick. All the windows are of the same kind of paper manufactured in Corea. It is very tough and warm. The windows of the palace, those of the great hall excepted, are composed of two parts, which are suspended by two hinges from above. The part either upper or under, or both, are in hot weather pushed out, and kept in that situation by a stick. This contrivance is the same at Rio de Janeiro for their outer doors. Houses have no cupboards and other conveniences ; and the tables are strong and clumsy, without drawers. The two tables across the ends of the hall are each thirty feet long, two feet four inches broad, and five and a quarter inches thick, each of one piece. All the columns and joists are also of one piece each. The throne and the tripods are of black ebony from India. Among the few articles furnished by the palace are a quantity of books, which, to appearance, are admirably written, and consist of numbers laid together into a kind of cover, which make a volume."

The Chinese had, on various occasions, shown much dexterity in cases of emergency. In the two large sheds erected at Hung-ya-yuen with the usual extraordinary despatch, for the protection of the presents, neither pins nor nails were made use of. They were composed of pines, tied with ropes, and covered with four folds of matting. The pines were rendered light, but brittle, by having the turpentine previously extracted.

A curious instance of Chinese ability occurred in cutting a pane of curved glass for the dome of the Ptolemaic system of the planetarium. The English artificers had twice failed in the attempt, when a Chinaman managed the business by the use of a red hot iron. The edge was not straight, but sufficiently so to answer the purpose. That great care must have been employed in packing the chests is

E

evident, for, on being opened after so long a voyage, and so many trans-shipments, scarcely any article had sustained the least injury. The fireworks, and even the glass, were all perfectly safe, with the exception of the cracked pane mentioned above.

The proper discharge of his duties occupied Dr. Dinwiddie's whole attention. He had just completed the plan of his operations ; had unpacked his own apparatus and books for future convenience, preparatory to those splendid exhibitions which, on the arrival of the Court, were to rivet attention in the wondering Chinese, when Government pressed the delivery up of a part of the presents yet in reserve. "This hurry seems to portend our departure from China. I am of the same opinion as formerly, that our stay will be short, and our opportunities few in this country. The extreme jealousy, added to the extreme ignorance of the Chinese, will prevent our visiting the manufactures, &c. Nothing but conquest by some polished nation will ever render this a great people. Their prejudices are invincible. Ask them whether the contrivers and makers of such curious and elegant machinery must not be men of understanding, and superior persons. They answer—' These are curious things, but what are their use ? Do the Europeans understand the art of Government as equally polished ? ' " "Writers," continues the Doctor, "represent the Chinese as the most mild and well-bred people on earth; that if two common mule drivers should jostle each other in a narrow way, so far from flying into a passion, they would assist and compliment each other on the way to some distance. We have experienced nothing of this character, but, on the contrary, the most violent fermentation of passions, throwing stones, boxing on the highway, frequent wrangling in the palace, and impudent boys. With respect to the filial piety and gentle manners, even of the lowest classes, nothing like their picture have we found in China. They have made out their description from Confutzee what ought to be, rather than what is. Carmen, in passing, use a common salutation, similar to *How do you do ;* and this only when acquainted with each other. When strangers, and running in each other's way, they scold as violently as in England ; but they are careful in driving ; always slow in passing another carriage, and constantly bawling out when moving along the streets.

From the day on which the Embassy passed within the threshold of the country, a feeling of fear or distrust seemed to pervade the motions of the Government. This feeling at the capital was too evident to be mistaken. A tent of soldiers constantly guarded the Palace, from which there was no egress but to be again immured at Pekin, where the apartments were also under the paternal care of other officials ready to check every step that dared to venture on forbidden ground.* Even the attention of the missionary interpreters was looked on with suspicion, and nothing could transpire but in the presence of a mandarine. Thus circumstanced, the gentlemen who were left in Pekin acted with great caution, and made as little show of curiosity or officiousness as possible. A similar policy did not seem to dictate others of the suite, for, on his Lordship's return from Tartary, it was with pain the Doctor saw parties herbalizing on the city walls, and taking such other liberties as could not but be offensive to the feelings of so strange a people as the Chinese. "The impetuosity of some gentlemen," says he, "will, I am afraid, do no little discredit to the Embassy."

Whatever ideas the Government might have entertained respecting the English, the people, as a body, were most absurdly prejudiced, and the arrival of the Embassy was made the subject of complete burlesque. It was announced in one of their daily papers that the English had brought *an elephant nine inches high; a parrot as big as an eagle; a hen which eat six bushels of charcoal a day; a man a few inches high;* and such other nonsense. But contempt, as in this case, was not the worst feeling, for when the Embassy was approaching Pekin, a Council was held, at which the missionaries were ordered to attend. They were asked whether the English were not a rough, outrageous people. After a little acquaintance, however, some of the Chinese admitted they had not found the English so uncultivated as they imagined.

The missionaries attended as interpreters, and at first were very obliging, but latterly seemed to get tired of their office. The life of a missionary here is a life of misery. Their labors are confined to the vicinity of Pekin, beyond the prescribed limits of which they dare not pass without the Emperor's permission. If a mandarine ask a watch, or anything curious the missionary has got from Europe, and is denied it, he will contrive to ruin the missionary by some means or other. The mandarines are but too often full of unlawful desires. An impudent instance happened at the palace, where a mandarine in yellow put his hand into one of the Doctor's

* Notwithstanding the great surveillance here pointed out, Barrow undertakes to describe the Gardens of Yuen-Min-Yuen as if he had travelled all over them. In the official account, Sir George Staunton, borrowing the language of Barrow, describes these gardens as "delightful," and about four square miles in extent. Subsequently, however, the "Travels in China" throws cold water on their beauty, while enlarging their extent to over thirty square miles; a clear proof the information was derived from any source but experience.

E 2

waistcoat pockets, and pulled out a penknife. He was about to repeat the experiment in the other pocket, when the Doctor thrust away his hand a little smartly, giving him to understand that only pickpockets committed such actions in England. "Jealousy prevails so much in this country, among the mandarines, that it is almost impossible for a very rich man to remain long in quiet possession of his riches. There are so many spies that nothing can escape them. Inferior mandarines are gaping for his office, and the Emperor for his cash. It frequently happens that the informer is rewarded by the office of the man he has been the instrument of removing. The missionaries find it very difficult to avoid being suspected."

The approach of the Emperor from Tartary summoned the Ambassador and suite so early as four o'clock in the morning of the last day of September, to meet him, according to etiquette, a few miles in the country. At a small house, near the appointed place, the gentlemen alighted from their carriages and horses, and walked the remaining distance to some tents, purposely erected for them. Here the military, in the shape of a troop of Tartar horsemen, were on duty. Lanterns, which, in China, are fashionable on all particular occasions, continued to burn in the broad light of day, conspicuous among the insignia of royalty. The gentlemen were afterwards drawn up in a line by the road side, and instructed in their obeisance to the sovereign of the Chinese empire, who arrived exactly at nine o'clock, in a sedan chair, not remarkably superb. His Majesty looked with seeming satisfaction on the gentlemen, as they made the required salutation on the right knee. The Colao, or first minister of state, with a considerable retinue all in yellow, the imperial color, followed behind. The English were conducted into the cavalcade to the house where they had left their horses, &c. Here they re-mounted, and separating from the cavalcade, returned to Hung-ya-yuen; but shortly after, at twelve, set out for Pekin, where they arrived at two p.m. In the meantime the Emperor proceeded to Yuen-min-yuen, where the instruments and other presents awaited his inspection.*

A different apartment of the palace had been appropriated to those instruments on which experiments were to be wrought, such as the air-pump, reflecting telescope, Parker's great lens, &c., all of which had only been two days delivered up. The lens was still unpacked, and the frame, or house, for exhibiting its powers, was

* Sir George Staunton, whose work is also full of disgraceful ingenuity, endeavors to make it appear that the gentlemen at the palace attended on the Emperor when he inspected the presents. Sir George endeavors to do this, though well aware none of the gentlemen were present.

of course not erected; but an attempt at erection was made on the
sly by two gentlemen who sometimes manifested a little officiousness. Apparently to make themselves conspicuous at the palace,
these gentlemen started early in that direction, October 1st, the day
after the Emperor's arrival, giving equivocal reasons for their visit.
Dr. Dinwiddie, learning the real object, applied to Sir George
Staunton, who procured a carriage, in which the Ambassador, Sir
George, and Mr. Plumb also rode to the palace. His Lordship's
object was to get some letters which the Colao had just received
from Chusan. These letters had been opened, and Diodati called
in to read them, but being written in English he could not. In
the hall, Gillan and Barrow, the gentlemen previously alluded to,
were found in a great bustle attempting to erect the lens-house.
The former, who undertook the business, did not remember a single
circumstance in the arrangement of the parts, and both took advantage of the opportunity to back out of the difficulty by returning to
town, leaving the Doctor with the workmen to superintend the
duties for which he alone was qualified. This and the following
two days were also devoted to experiments; but so soon as the house
was finished, the Emperor, carried in a plain " ist-ist," came from
the hall of audience to inspect it. " At that moment we turned
round the lens-house, and while I stood at the mirror had a full
view of his Majesty. He was very near us, and expressed nothing
observable in his countenance. His dress was much plainer, but in
the same manner as the first order of mandarines. He looked at the
lenses not more than two minutes, and retired. When viewing the
air-pump, &c., he said, *These things are good enough to amuse
children.*"

The air-pump and mechanical powers were selected for experiments, a variety of which were performed in presence of the chief
minister and a number of mandarines, who seemed little pleased
even with the most entertaining. When the lenses were ready for
experiments, the audience again attended, but the result only proved
that a Chinaman will entertain ideas truly provoking to a European
philosopher. Wood set on fire, even the Chinese cash melted by
the power of this apparatus, seemed to excite no other feelings in
the prime minister than lighting his pipe at the focus in derision of
its usefulness. A little mirth was occasioned by a eunuch who had
the curiosity to approach the focus with his finger, and felt more
than he had any desire for. Among other questions the Colao
asked: *How can an enemy's town be set on fire by the lens? How
will it act in a cloudy day?* At this juncture the oldest eunuch
made his appearance from the hall of audience, and, after several

hoas, " asked us to go and take down the lustres—that it was the Emperor's commands. This we positively refused to do ; and, being four o'clock in the afternoon, set off for Pekin, resolving for my part not to visit the palace again, nor contend with the most prejudiced of men." What probably contributed to this resolution was the fact, that Diodati had just told him that an order for their departure in a few days had passed in council, and was signed by the Emperor.

Next morning, an order arrived from his Majesty requesting seven men to repair to the palace, but the Doctor was firm in his resolution, and did not go. The officious gentlemen accompanied by the workmen went. They found the lustres already down and moved away ; the lens-house, too, was in pieces, and the two lenses lying on the pavement. On hearing this the Doctor exclaimed, " That lens—of which there is not an equal in the world —is consigned to everlasting oblivion." A great mistake appears to have been committed in furnishing the Emperor with a list of the presents, which he was extremely solicitous to have delivered up in full. The two gentlemen were asked to perform some experiments on the air-pump, but they refused, and only walked about till noon, when they returned to town, meditating on the storm that was brewing. The day which followed was October 5th, and at ten this morning suspense was put an end to, and the El Dorado dreams of the gentlemen blasted for sure, by the intelligence that they had only two days to prolong their stay in the capital. But few experiments, comparatively speaking, had been wrought, and these were entirely lost on this most prejudiced of people. The want of an opportunity of performing some on aerostation was much regretted by the Ambassador : though his Lordship mentioned the balloon, the diving-bell, and the fireworks, yet the principal mandarine heard the account without the least emotion or surprise. He was even indifferent to seeing the evolutions of his Lordship's guard, intimating that they already had the military manœuvres of all nations.

The mandarine who brought the order for their departure intimated, late in the same evening, that an additional grace of three days would be allowed to get properly prepared for the journey. Early the next morning, however, he returned to say that the first order must be obeyed. His apology was curious : *We told the Colao that two days more were necessary to get ready. He went to the Emperor, and the Emperor replied, You do wrong in detaining the Ambassador, for the cold weather will set in, which must distress him much on his journey.* The gentlemen, who had fondly indulged in the thoughts of passing the winter months at Pekin, felt a disappointment not easily conceived by so sudden a dismission. Their exertions, which had been somewhat relaxed at the prospect of a little more time, had now to be redoubled, putting them altogether into a state of indescribable confusion. The greater part of the night was devoted to other purposes than rest, and the little while the Doctor was in bed he could sleep none, owing to the disturbance occasioned by the preparations for to-morrow's journey ; nor did the bustle cease when to-morrow came. So peremptory indeed was the order that many things had to be sent off unpacked. Before their departure the Chinese servants were observed tearing off the silk, paper, &c., from the rooms.*

CHAPTER V.

DEPARTURE FROM PEKIN AND JOURNEY TO CANTON.

AT noon, on the 7th Oct., the gentlemen, emerging from the same gate by which they had entered, shook the dust off their feet, and turned their backs on the imperial city, where they had resided nearly seven weeks without one opportunity of seeing the place beyond the casual glance as the cavalcade moved past. They were now *en route* for Tonshu, which, short as the distance was, they did not reach till near eight o'clock in the evening. The shops, decorated with much painting and gilding, had then a beautiful appearance, being lighted by lanterns of various forms, made mostly of paper, but sometimes of silk and horn. Counters extended from one end to the other, with a passage in the middle, as is common in England ; and goods were neatly piled on the shelves. Their old apartments in the temple were ready to receive them, and as ready were the boats the next day to carry them down the river ; but these boats were much inferior in accommodations to those which brought them up with such flattering expectations. Dispatch was the order of the day, and another bustle ensued in getting the luggage on board, which was effected with hard labor. During the night-time the voyage commenced. The water was extremely low and retarded the progress of the boats, which were continually getting on ground.

---

* The extraordinary confusion into which the Embassy was thrown at this juncture, is entirely ignored by Staunton and Barrow, who are even willing to throw dust into the eyes of the public, by representing their treatment as all right. The confusion, however, is, to his credit, recorded by Eneas Anderson.

"To join the meanderings of the river by cross-cuts would render the navigation more expeditious; it would shorten the passage and deepen the channel, the bottom of which is gradually rising from the perpetual deposit of mud. But such canals would cut off a great extent of country, which is probably the reason the plan has not been adopted by the Chinese." Alluding to the yellow matter which this river is incessantly pouring down, it is further observed— "Where we left the Lion and Hindostan at anchor, at least fifteen miles from the shore, the vessels ploughed up the mud, though the sounding gave above twelve feet lower than the keel. The same thing happened off Chusan."

The Embassy, on its second arrival at Tiensin, Oct. 13, produced as great a crowd, and even more parade than transpired on the journey upwards. The theatre, however, had lost its attraction, and was apparently undergoing repairs. On the side of the river was erected a temporary larder, about fifty feet in diameter, having a quantity of meat ready dressed, besides fruit, &c., laid upon tables covered with crimson cloth, seemingly silk, ornamented with gold embroidery. No longer delay ensued here than was necessary to get the provisions on board. In three hours from their entrance the boats were a mile beyond the city, on another branch of the river, passing a square brick tower, about thirty-six feet in height, and about the same dimensions on each side of the base. On the flanks, in each merlon, were two square holes, and one of an irregular shape widening outwards. A door opened in front, about nine feet above the ground, arched in a curve between the semicircle and the Gothic.

The Lion and the Hindostan having sailed for Chusan, the Embassy had to be conducted thither, and for that purpose was placed under the care of a minister from the Emperor, who lost no time in pushing it forward to its destination. As far as Tiensin the travellers had only retraced their steps, but a new and extensive tract in the interior of the country was rising into view. The river on which they had now embarked, the Yuenlinho, was at first difficult to be distinguished from a canal, as the banks in many places had quite an artificial appearance, being formed of reeds or small bamboos, laid endwise to the river, mixed with earth, and fastened with pickets. Here, as on the Peiho, was seen a great quantity of earthen mounds. The water was in opposition, at the rate of two or three miles an hour, and quite as muddy as the Peiho, towards which it carried a respectable tribute of sticks, leaves, straw, and other rubbish. "This river winds through a level country in a most surprising manner, frequently turning off to one side, and then to the other, at right angles, which, as we

advance, become more and more acute. There are always two
bends in the river near each other, and in opposite directions, the
natural consequence of so flat a surface. Any angle casually made
must soon generate another in its neighbourhood, in an opposite
direction, as the current, by reflection, acquires an aim to the
opposite shore. Appearances seem to render it probable that the
angles here have been made in this way. Sometimes the windings
form a complete circle, and as the shipping in the river is considerable, the vessels have the singular appearance of sailing in all
directions upon the land."

Along the banks, on one hand or other, trees were generally met
with; the country, too, was well cultivated, and so full of inhabitants that villages were scarcely ever out of sight. One of these
villages disclosed a great many carts, and a vast quantity of bales
or packages lying at a short distance from the river. The square
brick towers were frequent. For two days after passing Tiensin,
they occupied the left bank, and then changed to the right. Houses
of an improved character sometimes made their appearance, and
among others a fine villa, with a beautiful gateway at the entrance
to the grounds, or demesne, was much admired. A week's sail on
the Yuenlinho is summed up with this observation : " Hitherto the
weather has been fine, the sky unclouded, but there is no variety to
be seen from the boats, compared with the banks of the Rhone, the
Thames, or the Manchester Canal."

As on the Peiho, all their motions continued to be directed by a
gong in the leading vessel. Though harsh when beat, it occasionally
produced some incomparably fine chords when played upon by the
stick dangling in the wind; and no doubt excellent music might be
drawn from such an instrument. " Our gong is nineteen inches
diameter, and one and a half deep at the rim, which is thin about
the edges."

The laborious industry of the Chinese peasant has a world-wide
reputation, and a striking instance occurred in " two men raising
water from the river by the use of an oblong vessel, to the brim
and also to the bottom of which two cords are attached. The ends
of the cords, which are from twelve to fourteen feet long, are held
one in each hand of the two men, between whom the bucket is
suspended. The water is a duct from the river. After swinging
the bucket towards the river—in its return it entered the water,
filled, and, resting about one second, by a sudden jerk of the rope
attached to the mouth of the vessel, they raised it nine or ten
feet; and when over the top they pulled the rope in the left hand,
which upset, and consequently emptied the bucket into a conduit in

the fields.   The bucket seemed to be half a parabolic spindle, about two feet long.   By this machine, the quantity raised at each time is not much, but the stroke is repeated at the rate of sixteen times a minute."

Religious ceremonies occasionally varied the incidents on the way, while the attention was much arrested by the military, who, at every little distance, were prepared with all the pomp and parade that music, colors, and other insignia could produce.   A more than usual display occurred at a village where the Embassy came to a dead stand for the unprecedented period of twelve hours.   This was occasioned by the baggage boats which, unable to keep pace with the others, had fallen behind ; but immediately on coming up the Embassy moved forward.

A majestic specimen of Chinese architecture was seen in a high pagoda rearing its lofty head near to the north wall of a large city now drawing near.   The pagoda is described in Ogilvy's Dutch Embassy, where it is said to be one hundred and twenty feet in height.   "It consists of nine stories, the lowest of hewn stone, and equal in height to one and a half of the others, all of which, as well as the dome, are built of brick.   A metal cover, with ring handles, is distinctly seen through the telescope."*

Close to this interesting structure is the town of Linsin, which was entered between two rectangular mounds of earth cased with large brick.   " The shell consists of a double wall, each the breadth of one brick, with some placed endwise to connect them together. The walls, at least the earthen part, are seen to extend on both sides of the river quite decayed, being composed of a kind of fine yellow sand of the same appearance as that on the banks of the river, and which, for some days past, has been flying about in great quantities, covering even the interior of the cabins with dust."

Shortly after the fleet had passed within the city walls, an accident occurred not very creditable to Chinese humanity.   Crowds of spectators continually flocked to the banks to get a peep at the uncouth strangers, every available spot being seized upon to gratify their curiosity.   At this particular occurrence, an old junk lying in the river was besieged.   " Part of the stern of this junk yielded to the weight of the spectators, a number of whom were thrown into

---

* In passing the pagoda, just mentioned, the barges never stopped ; nevertheless, Barrow assures us he got ashore, climbed the first story, and found the building inside choked with rubbish, without any means of ascending to the top.   In defiance of this, the subsequent English Embassy found the inside in beautiful preservation, with a staircase and stairs to the very top.

the river, and some of them in great danger; yet those out of the accident seemed not at all affected by it."

About three miles forward the boats entered the Grand Canal, a work of great magnitude, stretching through the finest provinces of China. It varies much in width, and there are no locks, as in European canals, the flow of water being regulated by flood-gates, consisting of planks fixed to slide up and down in abutments of masonry. Hitherto, the banks had not been less than twenty feet above the surface of the water, and now they rose higher, confining the prospect to the narrow range of the canal, where flood-gates, houses, spectators, and the military continued to attract attention. The canal was very serpentine, and presented one extraordinary bend, turning suddenly from a western to an eastern direction. By this time it was passing through ground not so level as formerly, and mountains were again seen ahead between the south and east. The summit was reached on the 25th, and on the morning following the current was running strongly in their favor, having previously been in opposition at the rate of 2¼ miles an hour. Lakes, villages, and industrial occupations united to form a succession of very pleasing landscapes. Like some other walled cities, Cining was approached after dark, which gave the Doctor occasion to remark: "The plan adopted seems to be—that we shall pass through the large cities always at night." The morning which followed (the 27th) unfolded very beautiful scenery—a large lake, it might be a succession of lakes, covered with fishing boats, and animated by a great number of villages on the borders: extensive level fields, too, where agricultural operations were going forward. In one direction the farmer was cutting down a tall grass or grain, in which scythes and rakes of a peculiar construction were employed. A field in another point of view exhibited three ploughs at work, each drawn by a bullock and two asses. One of the asses was sucked by a young colt. The plough had only one handle, held by the right hand, while the reins or halter were guided by the left. The share appeared thin and broad, and the whole very light—adapted to a soil easy of culture. A few corn ricks appeared of the same size and shape as in Scotland, only not so pointed, and flatter above the greatest width.

A large fortified city, the largest in appearance since leaving Tonshu, soon after brought to view a "prodigious quantity of shipping," a favorable specimen of the internal traffic of the provinces. Some of the junks were of the largest description, and many of them loaded with a black matter resembling coal. Here ships were built; and here, too, attention was drawn to a joss-house and deities, one of which was on horseback. A short distance forward the canal became very narrow, and full of shallows, which were pointed out by little sprigs, sometimes with red flags, rising above the surface of the water. The fleet was then drawing near a wall of masonry many miles long, and about five feet in height, fronting a massive earthen embankment, which separated the canal from a vast lake on the right, where innumerable fishing boats chequered the surface of the water. Various openings or sluices in the wall communicated with the lake, from which the water fell three or four feet into the canal. A little previous to this the current in the canal was running gently to the northward, but here it again became favorable, while less pleasing scenery succeeded as the lake disappeared. This however was only for a short time, during which a long grove of willows, cultivated in rows, presented a new feature in Chinese industry. The shallows in the canal continued, and the boats were frequently touching the bottom, but it was now spread to double its usual width, with every appearance of once having been a river, which, lying in the direction, had been taken advantage of.

In the vicinity of the Whangho, or Yellow River, the scenery again assumed interesting features, in which population and commerce shone conspicuous. Both sides were lined with shipping, villages, and trees; and several fine buildings stood prominent among the houses, which now generally had white walls, and were remarkable for neatness. Early on the morning of November 2nd, the fleet launched into the mighty river, which carried the vessels a considerable distance down before the crossing was effected. The passage is of great importance, and never entered upon without an offering to the dragon presiding over the river, which by far was the largest yet arrived at. It appeared a mile across, with a very rapid current, quite as full of mud of the same color as the Peiho.

On the south side the fleet again entered the canal, which still retained a natural appearance, and was regulated by locks of the same construction as formerly. The first gate entered, however, had a great descent, extremely dangerous for small boats. That in which Dr. Dinwiddie sailed was whirled by the eddy on the right bank, where it stuck fast for some time. Notwithstanding this, the gates on the whole seemed well adapted for the purpose; they were soon lifted, and easily adjusted to any height of water. Hitherto the opening of any of them never produced a change of more than three feet in the level, more frequently fifteen or eighteen inches. The planks are six to eight inches broad, and are drawn up by means of two ropes, one at either end, the other end of the rope being fixed to an axis, or round stick, put through two holes in two oblique stones placed on each side above. The abutments rise about ten feet above the surface of the water, and the passage between them is sufficiently wide to admit the largest junks.

Burying grounds in China seem to be very extensive. One in the neighbourhood of Tiensin was said to be sixteen miles in circuit. Near to the southern bank of the Whangho, attention was drawn to another, of large extent, full of tumuli, like the barrow on Salisbury plain, but rather more pointed. This may have been the case with the barrow, which probably are blunted by the great lapse of time.

In two hours from the burying ground the Embassy entered a spacious city, through which it was three and a half hours in passing. The neatness of the houses, the dress of the inhabitants, together with the great number of triumphal arches, the pompous manœuvres of the military, made a strong impression on the Doctor. This was Hoingan, a town of the fourth order. On the following day they rested before a walled town of the second order, where the canal was ten to twelve feet above the adjacent country.

For some days a great many strange-looking buildings lined the sides of the canal. From their shape they were, at first, on the banks of the Yellow River, taken for dwellings of a mean description, but were now ascertained to be bundles of a particular reed (cow-le-ang), made up ready for repairing any damage to the banks of the canal. With only the eye for an instructor, such mistakes will very easily arise; and it is as easy for a European to fall as wide of the mark as some of the Chinese, who, observing the lion and unicorn in the king's arms, imagined they were gods which the English worshipped.

The canal, spread to three times its usual width, continued much higher than the surrounding country, which, on the left, as far as the eye could reach, was laid out into extensive rice fields, sometimes entirely under water from sluices in the canal. On the right, a lake, or succession of lakes, appeared in the distance. Though wending its way through prospects always diversified by water, wood, and villages, the canal nevertheless kept on the outside of the large towns, exposing the suburbs only to view. Little of course could be seen beyond the towers and high walls by which they were always surrounded; and a circumstance which could not fail to excite suspicion was the fact of their being passed most frequently after night-fall. It was, however, in reserve, to be conducted during daylight through a large well-built town, with houses generally of two stories, the lower being occupied as shops. The windows above were large rectangular openings, with the frames suspended from the top, as usual. Some of the women spectators from the windows seemed to be dressed in petticoats, in a fashion not unlike Europeans. Houses in this province, Kiangnan, had chimnies rising above the roof, but more frequently placed on one side of the ridge. Some very favorable specimens of architecture added beauty to the vicinity, particularly two temples, the one circular, the other square, both supported on pillars according to Chinese fashion. There was also a pretty country seat, and perhaps not the least interesting, a large indescribable building near to a number of lesser buildings, all seemingly having some dependence on it. In their way through the town, the Embassy encountered a "prodigious quantity" of hay boats, two or three being joined together, and so loaded that the hay touched the water. Some distance forward another very extensive burying ground revealed a number of persons offering sacrifices. Here circular walls enclosed each a tumulus, or barrow, in the centre, to which there was an entrance. Some of the larger ones had archways under ground.

Since the passage of the Yellow River, a decided superiority was visible, not only in the houses, but also in the dress and appearance of the inhabitants, compared with the provinces of Petcheli, or Shantong. Everywhere throughout the journey crowds continued to flock upon the route of the returning Embassy, the more respectable classes having assumed their winter caps, while some of the country people still continued to wear the white turn-up bonnets, similar to those made use of by the sailors. The three-foot telescope was constantly in requisition to catch a clearer view of distant objects. Presenting it one evening towards a crowd, collected on the bank of the canal, "they all ran off, supposing it to be a gun, and being persuaded that the English, the most ferocious people in the world, think nothing of killing every person they meet with."

Poor as many of the Chinese are, begging appears so rare a circumstance amongst them that a solitary instance only is recorded. The mendicants, a woman and her son, in plying their vocation, made one prostration. All parties on board the junks were highly diverted at the close dress of the English, and laughed heartily at their manner of eating eggs; but what afforded the greatest degree of merriment was to see the gentlemen occasionally take a turn on deck, walking backwards and forwards, at which the sailors constantly burst into a fit of laughter. Such is the contrast of ideas that this useful and agreeable exercise was looked upon as the height of absurdity.

Either among the sailors, or the men employed in tracking the vessels, wrangling and other scenes of disorderly conduct occurred sufficiently often to show that human society is here pretty much alike what it is in other parts of the world. A fair set-to between two of the tracksmen consisted in seizing one another by the hair of the head, in which position the combatants remained bent down for some time, like boys. Neither would quit his hold till separated by an old man. An amusing quarrel, in which a female was the chief actor, took place on board one of the junks containing the apparatus. She was contending with her husband, the man at the helm, and maintained her part with all the virulence of a British virago. For some minutes she was lost sight off; but having only gone into the kitchen to light her pipe, as it appeared, she returned, smoking, to carry on the contest, to which seemingly there was no end. But bad behaviour of any description may find a parallel in China. One of the tracksmen was entrusted with money to buy some articles at a village, but instead of doing his duty he went off, taking with him some clothes belonging to his companions. A person that was sent after the rascal found him drinking samsu, and had him taken before a mandarine and committed to gaol.

When descending the Peiho a few instances of great irregularity occurred in providing the different vessels with provisions, some receiving too little, others more than their requisite quantity. The deficiency in these cases was no doubt accidental, and occasioned by the hurry to move forward. Eventually, however, the supply was not only regular and abundant, but the comforts of the gentlemen were even more attended to than on their arrival in the country. Wine and samsu continued plentiful, while two milch cows, each with a calf, formed part of the attendants, and had a boat to themselves.

"The sailors usually eat their breakfast at, or a little after, sunrise, dine at eleven, and again at five, seven, or eight o'clock in the evening. There is no distinction in the kind of victuals, which is the same at breakfast, dinner, and supper. They deal much in vegetable soups, rice, &c. Chinese cookery is not unpalatable: fish, in particular, is cooked extremely well. Charcoal of wood is the common fire used on board the junks for cooking, and the process of charring is much the same as in Europe."

The Chinese have no knowledge of the Sabbath, and their whole devotion consists in making three prostrations to their God; though they make nine to their Emperor. These ceremonies had already been witnessed at Yuen-min-yuen, and frequently on the journey. A sacrifice to Fo, on the 19th October, is thus described: "At daybreak two lanterns were placed at the head of the vessel, and a small tray, with three small cups, each about three-quarters full of shu.

Five small burning matches were then applied to a bundle of red and other party-colored papers. During the burning of this, a string of crackers was fired in order (as I suppose) to awaken the attention of the god. The whole was accompanied by a tremendous ruffle on the gong, sufficient to have aroused Morpheus himself. The captain made three prostrations to the burning papers, which continued to burn slowly away. He then took up one of the cups, and lifting it on a level with his forehead, with a pious stare at heaven, threw the contents over the head of the vessel into the river. The lanterns continued to burn for some time afterwards. In other vessels, instead of crackers, they used serpents, which produce a very loud report. The sound of all their explosive fireworks is much louder and shriller than any of the same size in Britain. On the papers offered in sacrifice are sometimes painted palaces, beautiful gardens, &c., which are all to be realised to the offerer in the next world. Some of the mandarines who were present looked with great gravity on the spectacle."

Fish, flesh, and fowl had been used on previous, as they were on subsequent occasions. The presiding deity of the Yellow River was thus propitiated. Though no notice is taken of any ceremony on the Blue River, two sacrifices, however, occurred the same day, subsequent to the passage. On the first of these occasions a cock and hen were killed on deck, over every part of which the blood was sprinkled. The other occasion, at four p.m., had the "usual oblations of burnt papers, and the gong; a tray with fish, flesh, and fowl; vinegar, shushu, rice, and oil. Each of the liquids were lifted to the mouth, then thrown into the water. A few grains of the rice were lifted with the finger, and also thrown overboard. Then a very small bit of the fowl, mutton, and fish, followed the other articles. This is the second day of the moon, which, I suppose, occasions all this extraordinary devotion. The captain prepared himself by washing his body all over, and putting on clean clothes."

Nothing in the whole journey continued so conspicuous as the military stations, with the soldiers drawn up in lines, sometimes a mile in length, always ready to honour the passing Embassy with a salute, which, in China, consists of three rounds. In firing their salutes, the guns are placed in a perpendicular direction to prevent accidents. The Chinese say, that *they level their pieces only at their enemies*. Linsin presented much military manœuvreing, which revealed some cannon mounted on carriages, and moveable on a swivel. The gun itself was not unlike a wall-piece. When passed in daylight, the soldiers displayed a variety in their uniforms; yellow, white, and blue were the prevailing colours. Among the insignia of their order, military trophies were frequent, and exposed with no little pride. The colours were triangular, with a loose white streamer flying along the hypothenuse. Music was generally struck up as a part of the services, in which trumpets, hautboys, drums, &c., joined to produce sounds not over pleasing to an English ear; yet at times the notes were soft, and somewhat resembled Scottish airs. In the night time the military presented quite an illumination, each soldier holding in his hand a beautifully colored lantern, the reflection of which, with the moon, on the smooth waters of the canal, produced a pleasing effect.

The country, which lately had been flat and sometimes swampy, became undulating in approaching the Yangtsekiang, or Blue River, which, at the crossing, appeared from two to three miles wide. This magnificent stream was entered at sun-rise, November 5th, and crossed in an oblique direction downwards, close by a small island presenting a beautiful specimen of those pagan temples which form the chief architectural ornaments of the country. "It crowns the summit of a mount about one hundred feet in height, and seemingly artificial. The pagoda itself is but five stories high, and terminates in a brass ball. Round the long spindle of the ball are seven or eight concentric rings, seemingly of metal, placed horizontally, that in the middle largest, diminishing both ways like the frustum of a cone. From the uppermost ring chains extend to the corners of the roof, in the middle whereof, and at the upper ends, hang bells which are made to ring with the wind. Bells also hang at the angles of the other projections below. A handsome open railing surrounds every story about one half the height."

"Beyond this beautiful island, in an angle of the river forming a bay, I counted no fewer than forty-two Chinese men of war, besides many others straggling in the river. In form, they are higher and narrower than the merchantmen, without any super-structure on deck, which is a clear curve from head to stern. The stern itself is flat, and adorned with various painted devices, but the sides above water are black, with a broad white line surrounding the port holes, which are rectangular openings about eleven inches by twelve. Each opening is shut with a lid, and there are exactly eight on one side, placed in a curve corresponding with that of the ship. Judging from the openings, the sides of the ship appeared to be very thin. The bottom is painted white, and, on the outside at least, the whole looks clean and neat. They have commonly two masts, with a great many flags. About forty men, dressed like the common soldiers, appeared on the deck of each."

F

Immediately on leaving the river, the suburbs of an extensive walled city (Chinkiang) furnished houses not only large, but having the appearance of elegance in their design. "Several junks on the stocks had all a side to the water, near which they were supported from fifteen to eighteen inches above ground. The supports, a row of which is placed along each side, consist of a number of pieces of wood, twelve to fifteen, or in some cases twenty-four inches long, and two or three inches square, forming a pile like planks laid out to dry. This I suppose is to facilitate the launch. Some of the supports are wrapped round with matting to prevent accidents."

Escaping from the last of several bridges leading into the city, another beautiful pagoda, on rising ground, came in sight. "It consists of seven stories, and terminates in an urn, something like a Florence flask, only pointed. The spindle has eight projecting arms of metal, on which bells formerly hung; the holes are distinctly seen through the telescope. This pagoda appears about ninety feet in height, and inclines a little to the left, the inclination beginning, at least is more apparent, from the fourth story, increasing upwards."

The passage of the Blue River, coupled with the pleasing scenery that followed in succession, made the most lively impression on the mind of our traveller, who says—"The beautiful variety of the morning sufficiently compensated for the rest of the day," for the canal afterwards was so sunk beneath the level of the country that they could see nothing of it.

Fishing is much resorted to by the Chinese for a living, and here in the interior, as well as on the sea coasts, the occupation is followed up to a surprising extent. Not only the canal all along, but every river and lake was swarming with piscatory operations. Some of the modes adopted are singular, particularly a board painted white, which is used for fishing by moonlight. Two boats, now passed in the canal, had on the gunwales of each eight or ten lawas, or fishing birds, drying themselves in the sun after having been at work. They were not tied, nor fastened in any manner of way. These birds, which are successfully trained to dive after fish, are said to be very numerous in China. Several days previously, during the twilight, large flocks of them passed over head in a northerly direction. They are black, and somewhat larger than the British crows, which they much resemble in their cawing. In the province of Kiangnan the net is more frequently adopted. "Four bamboos, joined at the top, and bent into nearly quadrants of circles, have their lower ends attached to the four corners of a net, which hanging below forms a kind of groin arch. This is let down by a rope and tackle into the canal and after remaining there for some time is suddenly drawn up, entangling the fish in the middle, or conical part of the net. A similar, but much larger net is used on the lakes."

Although every nerve was strained to keep the Embassy moving forwards, there were circumstances to contend with at times which rendered their progress slow. Tracking proved very troublesome from the foot slipping back in the clayey soil; and the current of the water, as well as the wind, was often strongly in opposition. In calm weather, or with a fair wind, the Chinese manage their junks well, but when the wind is contrary they can do little, having either to remain at rest, or adopt a tedious struggle called " edging with the single anchor." The boats have so little hold of the water that they are easily forced to leeward, and every time an opposing breeze freshened up two ropes had to be fixed to the prow to keep them from falling back, or towards the opposite shore. Passing a bridge with a strong head-wind was a work of difficulty, and in one instance was attended with serious consequences.

Few, if any, stone bridges had been seen spanning the canal till the passage of the Blue River was effected, when, all at once, they became numerous, forming entrances into walled cities. The road-way over these bridges is composed, however, of two flights of stairs impassable to wheel carriages. Bridges of only one arch were seen previous to reaching Chanchoo, the suburbs of which was entered under one of three arches, the middle arch being much the largest. Another bridge of similar construction occurred in the same town. The piers of these bridges were of one solid stone each, small below, but the workmanship displays a style of architecture corresponding nearly to other structures of the kind. The voussoirs are of very little depth, but longer in every alternate tier—those nearest the bottom about eight feet in length, diminishing to the key-stone, which is in no case distinguished. The arch resembles the Gothic rounded at the top. But also, in the same city, a bridge of one arch had the lower portion of the curve continued beyond the perpendicular tangent, or something like the horse-shoe. But bridges of another construction with flat arches were subsequently brought to light.

The embrasures and merlons in the walls of Chanchoo are like those of Pekin; but here, as in every other instance, not the slightest mark of cannon could be traced, nor in all the journey had a single ditch been seen to surround a walled city. From what little was observed, the houses seemed either built of black brick or painted black, a striking change to the cheerful white walls of other cities lately passed. A beautiful ornamental pavilion, with a roof like a sedan chair, and a pagoda of six stories, attracted considerable attention.

A short stage conducted the travellers to a large town, the seat of a cotton manufactory, or what appearances indicated as such. In their journey through it, numbers of long pieces of the cloth were seen hanging over slender wooden frames, not less than thirty-six feet in height. Considerable interest transpired with the occasion, but like various smoking brick-kilns, and many mechanical and agricultural operations, allowed only to be recognized in a passing glance. As most frequently happened at other important places, the boats did not even stop within its precincts.

A continued chain of towns or villages led to Sonshu, one of the few cities whose name transpired. The walls were undergoing repairs in several parts. " At an angle in the wall, the bricks are placed and varied in their position with the ends and sides alternately to the front. The embrasures are larger than formerly, something less than half the merlons, and not one foot thick. What is still more uncommon, the towers have but one embrasure in front, and one in flank. Between the city walls and the canal seventeen new ships lay upon the stocks, having their heads in this instance towards and near the water." But few cross-cut canals till now branched from the main trunk; here, however, the vicinity was everywhere intersected with branches, covered with innumerable junks. Bridges, more numerous than before, exhibited occasional peculiarities not previously seen, and amongst others those with the flat arches. Altogether the locality was one of variety and interest, only it was too near dusk.

In the middle of the night following the departure from Sonshu, the head of the junk struck against the masonry on the side of the canal, and violently shook everything on board. The vessel made water very fast, and the leak was stopped with difficulty. This junk, like every other, was unprovided with a pump, and when it made water, which it sometimes did, a large earthenware jar was deliberately filled below and carried up. Whether from the shock it had just sustained, or from some defect in the building, the junk was not altogether impervious to water above as well as below. Rain, which had seldom fallen in China, came down soon after in torrents, and made its way plentifully into the cabins. When pointed out to the captain he mended the chinks on the inside with red candles.

The next morning brought to view a number of small brick houses on the banks of the canal, and scattered over the rice fields to a considerable distance. These were the tombs in which the farmers of the fields were interred. " There are a few tumuli, but mostly those little black buildings, about five or six feet high, tiled, and quite in the shape of houses. Although not confined to any particular position with respect to the horizon, more appeared in an east and west, and a north and south direction than any other. In some the coffins are quite uncovered, lying on the surface, while the house serves as a case for them. The Chinese will not bury under water; hence the reason of raising little houses over the coffins, which are laid on the ground. Poor people, who cannot afford to build a house, leave the coffin to be exposed on the surface. Several were seen quite naked along the banks of the canal; and among them one which seemed to have received its contents very lately, as it was quite new."

Prospects of very pleasing scenery followed in close succession for some time. "About a mile distant, on the right, lies a considerable village or town, between which and the canal are several sheets of water, interspersed with beautiful islands. On the left, at fully twice the distance, another town and another lake equally claim our admiration. In short, the country is everywhere covered with villages, wood, and water."

The cultivation of rice, a great object in China, had all along attracted attention more or less. In some fields the young plants of a future crop were just rising above ground, overspread by a very shallow covering of water; while the crops of the present season had attained maturity, and presented a very cheering prospect. Reapers were occasionally busy cutting down fields of the grain, which was about two feet high. "The blade of the sickle is about five inches long, and one and a-half broad, fixed to a round wooden handle, at an obtuse angle. The edge of the blade turns downwards like a scythe. Five or six cuts fill the left hand, which is afterwards raised, and separated from the growing rice, solely by the left hand. It is then laid across the ridge, in a smooth even row, without any bands, which is an afterwork. When tied into sheaves, a bamboo stick is thrust obliquely into the side of one, near the band, and a triangle is formed of three sheaves, which are supported with the tops downward, an excellent contrivance for drying."

But these operations were now in a great measure to give way, and the agriculturist's attention directed to very different pursuits. The Embassy had reached the vicinity of those extensive mulberry plantations employed in rearing the silk worms, the most celebrated in China. The country, at least near the canal, became wholly covered with the white mulberry tree, from six to eight feet high, and two to four inches thick in the stem. Some plantations were entirely stripped of their leaves, contrasting forcibly with the luxuriant foliage of others.   Underneath, the ground was kept clear and in excellent order.   Such was the scenery that attended the arrival of the Embassy at Hanshu, on the afternoon of Sunday, the 10th November.

The same jealous caution which had conducted the Embassy to the capital was pursued in its return.   So strict was their injunctions that the captain of the junk in which our informant sailed received a flagellation for allowing Dr. Scott to go on shore.   This happened October 14th, while stemming the Yuenlinho.   However, shortly afterwards this severity was mitigated, and the gentlemen had the wonderful favor granted them to walk on the banks occasionally if they chose.   As they approached the ships, the Chinese, indeed, seemed to double their good offices, by paying greater attention in other respects; but in all this a deep laid policy, to smooth the disagreeable aspect of so sudden a dismission, was plainly visible. It came out on the journey that letters, written by the Ambassador, from Pekin, desiring the ships to wait at Chusan for the Embassy, had not been sent off by the Government from a suspicion that the letters required the ships to sail.   So great appears the anxiety of his Majesty to keep his English acquaintance at a distance.   Nevertheless, the Governor of Kiangnan, who met them on the way, remarked to the interpreter—" *That it was a shame to hurry men out of the country who had come so far to visit it.*"   This Dr. Dinwiddie sets down as " a piece of blarney, which costs little."   But how curious —the heads of the Embassy began now to look upon their treatment in the most favorable light by professing to believe that the Emperor meant to do the English service by sending them off so soon.   " Sir George asserted that the Chinese never allowed an Ambassador to remain above a certain time, being always sent away at the first proper season for their departure.   But was the 2nd of March a proper season for the Russian Ambassador's departure? and did not the Portuguese Ambassador dine with the Emperor at his private table?   If it be an established rule of the Court of Pekin not to permit an Embassy to remain beyond a certain period, why is it not mentioned by the writers on China?   Why was the circumstance not known to the English Embassy, who were in possession of all the books and every information on the subject? The truth is, every attempt at explanation involves the business in more difficulty, and renders it more probable that the behaviour of the gentlemen of the Embassy themselves was the principal cause of our treatment in this respect."

Immured at the capital, and afterwards hurried through the country, with hardly time to look at an object, the gentlemen had few opportunities for information ; but to increase their mortification, the want of a knowledge of the Chinese language rendered those opportunities of little avail. "In all our operations, no plan or system has been adopted; no regular orders given, at least adhered to. Our only interpreter, an ignorant, bigoted priest, without an atom of science, without curiosity or liberality, puts questions frequently different from the intentions of the proposer, either through ignorance or prejudice. We pass through the country like so many dumb persons, having no opportunities of asking or receiving information on the most common subjects."

Previous to their arrival at Hanshu, the termination of the Grand Canal, it was ascertained that the Lion had sailed from Chusan, a circumstance which left the Chinese the only alternative of conducting the Ambassador still through the interior all the way to Canton. The Hindostan, however, was waiting for its captain, who had accompanied the Embassy for special purposes, and arrangements were made for a part of the gentlemen to go with him. Doctor Dinwiddie joined the party to Chusan to take care of the apparatus, which circumstances rendered highly proper to send by this conveyance. The separation naturally occupied a few days, and during the interval, permission was obtained, through his Lordship, for the Doctor to walk a few miles into the country, among rice fields, and plantations of mulberry trees, and where also a great many tallow trees were cultivated. From the fruit of the latter is distilled an oily substance, which is extensively employed by the Chinese in the manufacture of candles. The fruit, which contains the tallow, is about the size of a sloe, at first green, but black when ripe, in which stage the rind or shell opens, leaving a little ball, very white, on the tree. The process of extracting the tallow is by boiling the bruised balls in water, when the oily matter swims on the top, and is skimmed off. A few plants were collected, and also some information respecting the rearing of the silkworm, in answer to a number of questions lately received from Lord Macartney.

Like every other city, Hanshu was forbidden ground, and the junks, which brought the gentlemen to its walls, still afforded accommodations during a short lived residence of three days, marked by hurry and bustle, as usual, in separating, packing, and sending off the baggage destined for Chusan. Upon the same day, 13th November, the two divisions of the suite took their leave of each other, and of the suburbs of Hanshu. His Lordship was taken in charge by a newly-appointed governor of Canton, while the party for Chusan continued under the guidance of their previous conductor, Sontagin. The latter party had the advantage of a few hours in the start, and after crossing the Green River proceeded by water as formerly, when something new in inland navigation came to light. The canal, or river, was banked across by an inclined plane of masonry down which the barges descended by their own gravity, at an angle of about forty-five degrees. The difference of level thus overcome was about ten feet. A second launch on the third day entered the river Linho, where other boats were in readiness to carry them to sea.*

From the first, the scenery on this route was beautiful, but for variety and sublimity now exceeded anything witnessed in China. A broad river, full of islands, winded its way through a richly-cultivated valley, beyond which, at different distances, rose several ranges of bold majestic mountains, exhibiting striking appearances of volcanic origin, and other singular peculiarities. At one point, we are told, "The varying shadows of the clouds passing along the sides of the fluted mountains; beneath the red tallow tree loaded with ripe fruit, mingled with the deepest evergreen; the fields waving with luxuriant crops of rice and culinary vegetables; villas and houses scattered around; close to the shore a long line of military decorated with colors and trophies; still nearer, the shipping in the river, with their flags and pendants variegated in the most brilliant colours: all taken together form the noblest scene I ever beheld." The scenery was still charming when lighted up, in a calm evening, by the full moon shining with unclouded majesty.

The military continued to be marshalled in large bodies, so near that one line was scarcely passed when another came in sight. Three salutes accompanied the usual display. For the space of five hours the vessels anchored off a long line decorated with three fine trophies. A large painted screen generally occupied a position near to the mandarine's trophy, and on the one now abreast of them was the figure of a huge tiger, about ten feet high and twenty-five long. The look-out towers, which lined the banks of the Grand Canal, did not cease here. When passed in the night, the sentinel beat his gong twice, beginning slow, and increasing with great rapidity each time. Two similar flourishes followed upon a wooden instrument.

Five soldiers attended as a guard, and conducted themselves with much propriety. As provisions were plentifully supplied, a part of the superabundance was one morning bestowed on the guard. The principal, who appeared more than a common soldier,

* In 1847, a few years before his death, Barrow (then Sir John) published his Autobiography, in which he re-produces his China travels. In this work, he places the contrivance of the *glacis* (inclined plane) on the Grand Canal, "between the two mighty rivers of China." To this every authority, including Barrow himself, gives a flat denial.

followed by the others, came a few minutes afterwards, and bending the right knee, gave thanks for the present. A mandarine, with a blue ball, was introduced on the way, and made the gentlemen a present of some oranges and sweetmeats. Immediately afterwards his looks bespoke a feeling that he expected something in return. Visits were received from several persons of distinction, and among others, one with a brass ball seemed much surprised at the Doctor's dress. He also signified that it was very improper for a man of his (the Doctor's) years to shave his beard.

The river increased rapidly to three times the width where first entered, but unfavorable winds and rapid flood tides prolonged the passage, which towards Ningpo was very troublesome. To over-come these obstacles some bad manœuvreing happened, by which two of the vessels ran foul of each other three different times. After this a system of alternate moorings was adopted, and proved evidently a better plan. "The junks are of the same construction as those formerly seen off Chusan, and are provided with wooden anchors. In heaving the men stand on both sides of the windlass; when one has pulled down his handspike he pushes it through to his comrade on the opposite side, and thus on alternately. The wind-lass is ill made, having the cheeks parallel to the sides of the vessel instead of to each other, which occasions two gaps between the windlass and cheek. Cables are made from cane grown in a distant part of the empire."

Before sunrise on the 18th they passed the walls of the city of Ningpo, "once known to the English, and where, in all probability, but for their bad behaviour, they might have had a factory still." On both sides of this city very long lines of military were drawn out, proving unquestionbly the paternal care which the Emperor exercised over his guests, and very probably also to keep the same guests in mind of his irresistible power. At some distance below, in front of another line of soldiers, the boats anchored, being detained till the return of the tide, which was very rapid. It was the day of full moon, and the tides rose seven or eight feet perpendicular. Here the river is as wide as the Thames, and as muddy as the Peiho.

At the bottom of the river, and in sight of the sea, the conductor, who had all along behaved in the most creditable manner, signified his intention to return, and made each of the gentlemen a number of presents in the Emperor's name. For this they made the usual obeisance, by bending the right knee before a large picture placed to the north. The presents consisted of *a large parcel of tea; two cylindrical baskets of the flowers of tea, the finest that grows; eight pieces of black nankin cloth; four pieces of white flowered silk; a bundle of raw silk, and ten parcels of tobacco.* The gentlemen had all alike, and the servants a third or fourth of the same quantity. With further presents from himself, and two hearty shakes of the hand, Sontagin took his leave. " We were sorry," adds the Doctor, " that he did not accompany us to the ship. He is a polite, well behaved man."

Foul winds and an agitated sea detained the junks at the entrance to the river, which was strongly fortified by nature, and might easily be rendered impassable by a few batteries. These could be so placed that every ship entering would be exposed both to a direct and raking fire within less than half point blank. A high rock, on the right hand entering, supports a square tower, from which, and also from two men of war lying below, guns were fired several times. Not one gun, however, was seen mounted in an embrasure in all China.

The first favorable opportunity for the junks venturing out enabled the gentlemen once more to set their feet on a British bottom, of which they felt not a little glad, having had quite enough of their dumb travels. Yet, while the Hindostan was taking in her cargo at Chusan, our traveller was permitted to land again, and for once had the opportunity of being conducted through the streets of a Chinese city, and making observations unmolested. The streets are very narrow, and the walls enclose about three times the quantity of land built upon. A square tower defends the gate, and is hollow, with a magazine inside. The ramparts are eight feet broad, and embrasures one foot wide within, but double that width without. Another square tower near the hospital has embrasures twenty-two inches wide, with merlons thirteen inches thick below and eleven above. Some columns here have a globe of stone for a pedestal.

A variety of machinery that came under review proved that the Chinese, in some instances, were centuries behind the nations of Europe. The following are among those particularized :—

" A machine for weaving mats consists of an upright frame, with small fibres along it, through a piece like a weaver's *slae*, by which the longitudinal fibres are crossed over the latitudinal, put in singly by a boy. A handle is fixed to the moveable *piece* which serves both as a *slae* and *heddle*. It both crosses and strikes the fibre put in close to the other."

" A smith's bellows is formed of a square box, rather deeper than broad, with two valves in the front opening inwards. The handle is composed of two pieces of timber, joined by a cross piece near the ends. The blast is weak, but nearly continued, and only interrupted for a moment at the change of direction." As to the position of the other valves and form of the interior, the imagination was left to its own exertions to follow out particulars.

" The upper stone of a mill, for grinding rice, is about twenty inches in diameter, and four or five thick. In the eye of this a conical hopper of matting is fixed—it consequently turns with the stone. Round the stone is a frame of wood, to which is fastened a short lever. The power, a bullock, applied to this lever, puts the upper stone in motion, and turning in this slow manner on the under stone grinds the rice. The ground rice falls from every part of the circumference, like the Scots quarries. A sieve, placed horizontally is moved backwards and forwards by a jointed lever, and separates the meal from the bruised grain." Neither wind nor water mills for grinding corn, or for any other purpose, was seen in the whole journey, which strongly corroborated an observation of one of the missionary interpreters, that there were none in China."

" A shelling machine consists of two *stones*, or rather blocks of wood, the under a complete solid circle, the upper a ring of the same diameter, from twenty to twenty-two inches. The ring is about four or five inches broad, and teeth are cut in both, along the radius, sloping as in a saw. The ring, or upper *stone*, is turned by a lever of five or six feet, a hole in the end of the lever being fixed on a pin on the upper side of the ring near the circumference."

" A machine for breaking cotton seeds is as follows : An iron spindle, about a foot long, and three-quarters of an inch diameter, is placed horizontally above a wooden cylinder of the same length, and an inch and quarter in diameter. On the farther extremity of the iron spindle is fixed a cross of wood, each arm fourteen inches long with *weight* on the extremities. Near the centre of the cross is a pin, which receives the noose of a line, the lower end of which is attached to a pedal, and moved by the foot. A winch is applied to the lower wooden spindle, and turned by the hand. The cotton, in small quantities, is passed between the rollers, and the seeds bruised."

" A pump is a trough, or conduit, in which runs a wooden chain with rectangular lifters placed obliquely. The lower half of the chain runs in the conduit ; the upper half slides down the curved surface of a split bamboo. The chain works upon two rollers about four inches in diameter, placed one above, the other below. On the ends of the upper roller are fixed two levers at right angles to each other, and in the extremity of each a pin goes into the handle The position of the levers at right angles is agreeable to mechanical principles, and not followed in Britain. The pump is sometimes wrought with the feet, in which case the roller at the upper end has an axis, through which spokes are passed, with broad pieces on the ends whereon the man treads, while holding a cross-stick or rail. The quantity of water raised is small."

"A plough is constructed with one handle, beam, sheath, narrow head, and thin triangular share, with a piece placed very little obliquely to turn the furrow slice, which is cut entirely from the bottom and lifted over. The share is about eleven inches long, and nine broad at the base. There is no culter. The beam is about six feet long, and much bent. Only one horn. The handle, to the mortise of the beam, is thirty inches, and between the beam and head nine inches. The head is three feet long, and two and a half inches thick, with a pin on the side."

"Fanners are exactly of the same construction as those of Britain, only with one eye, and open directly behind, and not above. The hopper is square, and fly with four vanes."

Sickles, drags, hedge-hooks, and various other implements of lesser importance had generally some peculiarities in their form. Mirrors made of metal were a little convex, and well polished. Copper and brass wire seemed in abundance; and what was looked upon with some degree of curiosity, were several pieces of velvet, which, however, might have been of European manufacture for any thing known to the contrary. Beds, like British post beds, had double posts in front, round and slender. The land unbuilt upon was neatly cultivated. A field of clover had the plants in rows across the ridge; a crop of rice had previously been taken from the same field. Many plants of the tallow tree were cultivated here.

The next day, the 30th November, the Hindostan got under weigh, leaving its track upon the water by a long train of yellow mud. Inside, the harbour of Chusan is safe, but rather difficult of access, and in the middle of the narrow passage leading out, the bottom of the ship struck upon an unknown rock, but she soon righted herself, without occasioning any material damage. Outside, and fairly clear of the islands, the swell of the sea was prodigious, and this disagreeable motion was further increased by a hard gale which ensued for several days. It was very alarming during the second night, and the morning which followed brought but little comfort—rain, darkness, and a tremendous sea. The foresail was shivered to pieces, and they continued under bare poles, for the safety of which great precautions were adopted. Towards the third evening the gale began to abate, and finally to soften into a prosperous breeze, which brought them safe within the Bocca Tigris. The scenery was peculiarly Chinese. Besides this celebrated fort, presenting twelve guns in one front, it was rendered highly interesting by various other islands of the most romantic shaped land. Here, too, the river was thick, and mud was raised by every motion of the vessel. The pilots seemed extremely ignorant of the channel, the bottom being touched several times before reaching Whampoa, where a mandarine in blue came aboard, but previously saluted with his gong, and had the compliment returned from the Hindostan by three cheers. On the following day, December 12th, the Doctor set out in the pinnace, and, just a week before the Ambassador, arrived in Canton, where apartments were provided for him at the English factory.

CHAPTER VI.

RESIDENCE IN CANTON.

In this commercial metropolis of the far east Doctor Dinwiddie was fully impressed with the idea of delivering a course of lectures; and before their separation, at Hanshu, he waited on Lord Macartney, who kindly granted permission to use any part of the apparatus necessary for that purpose. The disposition of the English residents was found favorable, and the lectures, which did not commence till after the Ambassador's arrival, were well received. They were attended by Europeans, and such of the Chinese as knew a little of English. One of the natives, with a mind better fitted for commercial transactions than the study of philosophy, and fancying all this exhibition was the prelude to a sale, asked the Doctor how much per cent. he intended to make by his goods. The ideas of a Chinaman are often strangely contrasted with those of a European. Dining one day where a Hung merchant was in company, the merchant, although he seemed to have very clear ideas of Doctor of Medicine, could not easily comprehend the meaning of Doctor of Laws. He asked the philosopher *what weather it was going to be? Whether, without rising from his seat, he could remove a certain picture from the room?*

The Embassy was naturally the subject of much conversation, giving rise to such observations as these :—" Three months' negotiation was unavoidable to get over the necessity of Lord Macartney travelling all the way from Canton. At length, on the Commissioners declaring that, but on condition, he would not proceed at all, the Emperor consented to allow him to land at any port he chose, and a guard of three hundred men were appointed to attend him. These were in readiness at every port on the east coast for near three months. The Commissioners were much afraid that the Emperor's patience would be worn out, and were much at a loss to learn the reasons of our delay at Rio de Janeiro, the Straits of Sunda, and Turon Bay. The despatches were ready at Batavia on our arrival, but the commanders insisted they could not enter the Chinese seas before the end of April. Could they not have made Macao and relieved the Commissioners from the anxiety which they felt respecting the disposition of the Emperor, so long disappointed, and so little accustomed to such treatment? Why not accept of the Tartar Legate? He was probably sent by the Minister as a go-between the Ambassador and his master. Why not bribe him? All agree that the Minister is one of the most corrupt men in the empire. A public present he cannot receive, but he expected something considerable in a private way. Is he accessible? Every man is so. To have had any good effect on the Chinese, the guns ought to have been of a larger calibre. It was very improper to present young Staunton to the Emperor; he ought not to have been presented at all. What must the Chinese think of the English, who make their boys men before their time ? "

"Letters received from the missionaries at Pekin mention the following reasons for Lord Macartney being sent off so soon:—1st, not complying with the ceremonies of the country ; 2nd, not bribing the lower mandarines ; and 3rd, one mandarine being degraded one button on his Lordship's account."

No immediate benefit seemed to result from the Embassy regarding the objects complained of, and particularly since its arrival in Canton, the Chinese authorities were very strict. Walking one day in the fields on the opposite side of the river, where the Ambassador resided, the Doctor had the curiosity to pick up some indigo of a smaller species than that cultivated in India, when he was immediately challenged by the military who acted on his Lordship's guard. This did not use to be the case previously, nor was it the only instance of the kind that occurred to himself, but more than ordinary severity was observed with regard to boats passing up and down the river.

" The Chinese are not likely to make any alteration in our trade. It will always find its own level – can never be forced. No advantage seems to arise from having a port to the northward, on account of the cheapness of carriage and freight. The market is already overstocked. If the Chinese wish our manufactures they will have them at Canton, or anywhere ; and it is presumed that the difficulties attending the navigation of the eastern coast of China, with the general shallowness of the water, will more than overbalance all other proposed advantages.''

" The English carry on seven-eighths of the European trade of Canton. Tin, lead, copper, and cloth pass for money in China. These articles of the English company are understood as such, for the bales, &c., are never opened by the merchant here, but sent through the whole empire, even to Pekin itself, in the original packages. But the Chinese merchants will not answer for their teas without examination. A number of boxes are opened, *ad libitum*, and if, on their arrival in England, it is found that any others are bad, they are sent back to the merchant here, who always receives them, or makes a proper deduction if only an inferior kind of tea. There is no country in the world where trade is carried on so expeditiously as at Canton. No duty is paid either by the exporter or importer ; all is paid by the Hung merchants, and included in the price of teas. By this means the company are freed from much imposition, and the business of clearing out, so troublesome in England, is here entirely avoided. Every regulation is calculated to avoid smuggling and promote expedition. Duties are laid on, in general, with much judgment. Watches, and other small articles, which may be easily smuggled, pay no duties except fees of office ; but bulky articles pay a high duty. The cotton duty is low, because cotton is manufactured in the country.

" At present the Hung merchants owe great sums of money to the English, and are much pressed for more. The Chinese will not trust one another; hence the advantage of supercargoes lending them money, which commands from twenty to twenty-four per cent. The Hung merchants are very punctual in their engagements, but the recovery of debts, in general, is very difficult. If the debtor be a high mandarine, it is extremely so."

A great want of prudence seemed to prevail among all the European establishments in cases of fire. '' Between four and five one morning the flames burst out very strong in the Swedish factory, to which a number of engines were brought with difficulty. None of them played well but the Dutch engine; all the others were out of working order and some of them in very bad repair. It seems strange that little or no water was available in the factory, and this the more as water is always found at a few feet deep. Open wells with a tube to fix the feeding hose on, to prevent the engines choking, would be useful in a place that is frequently subject to fire ; or a pipe might bring water from the river sufficient for all the factories. But one of the most important desideratums is the want of a large fire proof to secure books, papers, and things of greatest value."

Canton proper is a walled city, at some distance from the river, but between the walls and the river are extensive suburbs, supplied with shops of every description. These suburbs only are accessible to Europeans ; and they proved very interesting to Dr. Dinwiddie, who devoted the opportunity now offered to collecting specimens and information on Chinese manufactures. He seems to have been persuaded that China would be an attractive subject for future lectures ; and, apparently, with this in view, he was frequently out shopping, making purchases, but principally to inspect the tools and *modus operandi* of different tradesmen. Abundance of articles useful and ornamental met the eye at every step ; and though some ideas might have been derived from the influx of Europeans, an originality peculiar to the Chinese was too apparent to be mistaken. Among other curious purchases was a clock of a most singular construction, "the clock itself being the pendulum, while the pallets of the common form were connected with the stand." It was entirely the work of a skilful native, whom the Doctor instructed in filling barometer and thermometer tubes, and some other properties useful to his profession. The mariner's compass is of great importance in China, where it was in general use long before it was known in Europe. Although the Chinese have made many discoveries in the arts, it is singular they should have no instrument for taking the sun's altitude, nor any other nautical instrument but the compass, which is divided into twenty-four points, a more convenient division than thirty-two. Spy-glasses and spectacles enter largely into the catalogue of Chinese manufactures ; the latter, however, are badly constructed, with lenses from two to three inches diameter, by which they admit too much side light. They are fixed by passing a double thread over each ear. Among the purposes to which metal is applied is the singular one of being manufactured into mirrors, which are sometimes of large dimensions. They were exceedingly well polished, and many of them curiously figured in relief behind. Watch and other small frame glasses were cut by an instrument of steel with great ease, and without any noise. A boy ornamented Chinese locks very rapidly by a punch. Oil and emery were in common use in polishing, cutting, drilling, &c., as well as many other ingredients employed in England.

Some beautiful specimens of painting occurred, among immense varieties having only curiosity to recommend them : but nothing remarkable in the way of sculpture seems to have drawn the attention. As modellers, however, Chinese artists have attained to great eminence, their figures being perfect imitations of nature. Much time and patient perseverance is devoted to ornamental carving, many of their works in this line being exceedingly difficult, and at the same time so exquisitely performed as to be above all praise. Curiosities in endless variety, and often ingeniously contrived, is another grand branch of Chinese industry. The following specimens formed part of the Doctor's collection, which included an extensive assortment of tools, implements, pictures, casks, models, &c. One piece combined a bird, a bow, and a pea. By a curious contrivance, the bird pulled out a small peg, when the bow discharged the pea perpendicularly upwards, which the bird immediately flew after and catched. Another piece exhibited a dog watching a pear on a tree. When the pear was removed the dog began to bark and continued barking till the fruit was replaced, when it instantly ceased. A very ingenious figure, representing a writer or draughtsman, was contrived to copy writings or drawings very neatly. The figure moved from one part of the machine to the other with great ease, and very naturally ; and the first productions of his pencil required by the Doctor were the King and the Prince of Wales. But apparently the most amusing was the person of a little conjuror, with a book in his left hand and a wand in his right, discovering what picture was placed into a small drawer. " There are sixteen pictures in all, any one of which is put into the little drawer, and the drawer closed. The conjuror first makes three bows ; then lifting up the book, and waving the wand twice, looks attentively at the former. Upon raising the wand to a little door in the upright part of the machine— the door flies open and reveals the same picture which was put into the little horizontal drawer. Another signal is made with the wand, and the door shuts. Should you attempt to cheat him, by putting no picture in the drawer, he shakes his head twice, and proceeds no further."

Jugglers, *in propria persona*, were frequently performing the most dexterous feats with rings, cups, balls, &c. Two brass musical instruments, like plates, were wheeled, one on and in the other, in a number of ways truly wonderful; and in one instance were supported wheeling on the end of sticks held nearly horizontal. Rings were joined and disjoined in a surprising manner. This appeared exceedingly difficult. A female character was once so well supported that it was impossible to have known that the person was in reality a man. The juggler talks only to one person, who stands by and pretends to direct him. This seems better than in Europe, where he is perpetually teasing some of the company with his impudent jargon. Besides the trades and professions most common in other countries—even that of the law was supported by a high mandarine established at Canton.

G

The suburbs of the city were interspersed with fields of indigo, rice, and various culinary vegetables, among which a walk formed a very agreeable recreation. Two different species of vegetables were frequently planted on the same ridge, such as petsy and turnips, peas and leeks. " Peas, only lately introduced into Macao, were for some time carried to Canton at a great expense. The farmers here, finding a good market, now cultivate them in considerable quantities, and stick them as in Europe. Though in the middle of winter, we have green peas every day to our dinner." The table at the factory, it may be mentioned in passing, was most sumptuous, and said to cost the Company upwards of four thousand pounds a year.

The fine mansion of Fanliqua, a rich native, offered an occasional retreat to Dr. Dinwiddie. " A pond in the pleasure grounds is full of golden fishes with beautiful white fins. By tapping on a board they all came expecting food. Ladies frequently exercise themselves in fishing here. When a fish bites—the rod is thrown into the water, and a man is sent in for both the fish and rod. The rod is furnished with a winch not unlike those used in Britain." Most of the fruits peculiar to eastern climates were cultivated here, and some of them particularized as extraordinary in their appearance, such as the citron, large and yellow, with the top spreading out like the fingers of a man's hand. A fondness for luxury was everywhere visible. The bedrooms were not only excellently arranged, but the beds were scented, and hung with most beautiful curtains. Fanliqua had, moreover, acquired a taste for the fine arts, particularly music, of which he was fond, and occasionally indulged his guests to a tune on the Chinese organ, which played slow and rather pleasing airs. Portraits of the king and queen of England had a place in his collection of pictures. His antiquities were many, some of them said to have been in the family a thousand years. " A large candle, covered with gilt paper, four feet long and three inches diameter, burns before his father's coffin, which he has kept past him these five years, since his father died. Fanliqua's father resided some time at Manilla where he was obliged to turn Christian. When he left the island, and was at sea still in sight, he took the cross from about his neck, and tossed it into the sea, saying, it might go to Manilla where it was so much admired."

" However superstitious the Chinese may be deemed, they possess one convenient quality—they never interfere with strangers about religious matters. Their worship never interferes with their labor, being performed generally very early, before sunrise, or late in the evening after work. Divine service occurs at stated times, and is always celebrated with hymns and musical instruments, played on by the priests. Their religion is sprightly—nothing of the gloomy in it. In all countries the priests live well, and here they have spacious gardens belonging to the temple. The Chinese are also more liberal than most Europeans in permitting strangers to bury amongst them. In this respect, the tomb of Lopez, the missionary, is here an object of some interest to foreigners."

In no country, perhaps, do popular errors and prejudices prevail so much as in China. The Chinese Government is here considered the only antient and perfect Government on earth. The Chinese believe themselves the only really enlightened people, and that all other nations are barbarous; that China is situated in the middle of the earth, and all other countries scattered round it. An eclipse is occasioned by a great dragon in heaven getting hungry and seizing on the luminary, which he holds between his teeth till induced to quit his hold by the beating of drums, gongs, &c., made throughout China. If a house is struck with lightning—it is a sure sign the inhabitant is a sinner. A handsome man consists in being lusty—able to fill an elbow chair. A woman cannot possibly be handsome without small feet. Persons of the same name must not intermarry. The Chinese paint two eyes on the prow of their boats, under the belief, *if they cannot see—how can they know?* But the catalogue might be enlarged to a volume, embracing some ideas so outrageous to common sense that it is surprising they should meet with a general assent. For instance: we are told in the province of Xensi is a hill called Taipe, on which, if a drum be beat, thunder and lightning immediately follows; and, consequently, the magistrates have forbidden all persons, on pain of death, to beat a drum on the mount.

Remarkably fine weather attended the Embassy in Canton for some weeks after its arrival. About sunrise it was generally a little cloudy, but soon cleared up. "There is always a great degree of dryness in the air when the wind is northwardly; furniture opens and cracks in a surprising manner. On the contrary, when the wind is south as great a degree of moisture prevails and everything swells." The latter part of the time was marked by an almost uninterrupted succession of wet weather, which, however, was seldom very heavy. The thermometer at sunrise sometimes rose above sixty degrees, and only once fell so low as forty-three, when it proved a most miserable cold day.

The Ambassador arrived in Canton, December 19, and took up his residence on the side of the river opposite to the factories. Here he still lived at the Emperor's expense, and was protected by the Emperor's myrmidons. Apparently he moved very little about; on Christmas day, however, he dined at the English factory, where the whole suite and others, amounting to about sixty gentlemen, sat down to dinner. Altogether, his sojourn in Canton scarcely embraced a period of three weeks, for on January 8, attended by the whole suite, he descended the river to Whampoa, where the Lion lay at anchor. His Lordship was ahead, and, accompanied by the captains' boats, the procession had a fine appearance. The salutes of the Lion were most deafening, and it was amusing to see the Chinese stopping their ears. But the final departure of his Lordship was not yet fixed, and Dr. Dinwiddie, who had only commenced his course of lectures, returned the next day to Canton, where he remained the only gentleman of the suite till the 22nd of the following month, when he was summoned to join the Embassy at Macao. The friendship experienced in Canton was the source of much after pleasing reflection, and he left it with no little regret to prepare for Calcutta, where the Ambassador wished to send, under his care, some plants and other articles collected in China for the Governor-General of India. The boxes, in which the Doctor's apparatus and collection of curiosities were incased, were likely to be roughly handled by the Chinese authorities before they could be passed the Chop-house. The intercession of his friends, however, got the matter settled by barely opening the lids of two cases. It is observed that "wine had on this occasion a good effect." The Doctor was most timorous in regard to a gong, in his collection, which the laws of China prohibit from exportation. Besides the apparatus, the chop contained thirty-one chests of tea. It started in the evening, and by nine the next morning was alongside the Hindostan, lying some distance below Whampoa. Before the boxes could be got aboard they had to undergo another examination, but " the inspecting mandarine, although within hail, never made his appearance for a full hour. When he did come he simply looked round for about two minutes, and left us to get aboard the Hindostan without further molestation."

The scenery on the river, naturally beautiful, is improved by extensive shipping and cultivated fields, and no less by numerous elevations crowned by pagodas of a different construction from those in the north. The Hindostan was now lying near a famous quarry on shore, where the Chinese have from time immemorial been accustomed to dig long stones for bridges and stairs. Advantage was taken of the delay to visit it. " The rock is split into slices of the proper breadth and thickness, by iron wedges, driven in a line at three or four inches distance from each other. A small groove is cut joining the wedges ; water is then said to be poured into the groove, and after a short interval, it is affirmed the slice splits off straight. It is sometimes upwards of twenty feet in length. The rock seems a volcanic production, in which flints, quartz, and a great variety of matters are blended together. It is hollowed in some places into caves; in others, it is cut through into smaller and larger openings. The walls of some old houses near by are composed of a matter extremely like the rock. but artificial. Small pieces of the rock are united into a firm mass by a mortar composed, in a great measure, of sand."

On the third day the Jackall arrived, on board of which the Doctor descended to Macao, where he waited upon the Ambassador respecting the despatches for Bengal. The articles placed under his care consisted of several cases containing a number of tea, tallow, and varnish plants, besides a quantity of eggs of the silk worm. The introduction of these valuable articles into India was expected to be attended with the most beneficial results. On opening the paper that contained the eggs about half a dozen worms were hatched, and more than one-half of the eggs in a state that predicted a speedy birth. In a letter to Sir George Staunton, he says, "I am of opinion that it will be for ever impracticable to carry eggs from China to Bengal at this season of the year. March and April are the usual months of hatching in most parts of the world; even in England the worms are out by the 20th, or end of April, when the thermometer is at least ten degrees *below* what it stands at present. This experiment can only be expected to succeed when the eggs are sent off in November or December, and some notice must be taken of the failure, otherwise it may be supposed to have been owing to my negligence. The plants are seemingly in a good way, and, unless we are very unfortunate in weather, I have little apprehension on their account. I keep a thermometer in one of the chests, by which I regulate the opening and shutting of the cases."

Two-thirds of the population of the island of Macao were reputed to be Chinese, the other third chiefly Portuguese, whose trade, once flourishing here, was now greatly on the decline. "Although the columns of the Senate House proclaim the surrender of the island, the Chinese authorities treat the Portuguese with much contempt, exacting not only the duties of their own people, but also one-half of those of the Portuguese."

Attached to the house in which Lord Macartney resided was a beautifully romantic garden, which has received a classic celebrity from the cave in which Camoens wrote his poem of the *Lusiad*. A joss house, in the form of several curious temples rising one above another, brought to view several Chinese seamen in the attitude of making offerings. As Dr. Dinwiddie entered, one of them remarked with much simplicity, *I believe the English no savey much about religion.* A very great show of sanctity prevails here among the Portuguese—priests, churches, and crosses, continually meet the eye. On the citadel are two flags with a cross between them, as if the latter could be of any use in the defence. Ash Wednesday was devoted to active purposes on the part of the church. At four o'clock in the afternoon a long procession commemorated the occasion. " Death, with his scythe and roll, marched in front : next, a person in black bearing a large cross, showing the holes of the three nails stained with blood. The Virgin Mary, Jesus Christ, and a great many saints were borne in succession, while flags, crosses, bells, &c., intermingled with the long catalogue of figures, which were each placed on a bier covered with black cloth."

A few hours afterwards a striking contrast occurred in a procession of Chinese fishermen bearing lanterns, and transparent fishes, illuminated, and accompanied with music, gongs, &c. " The fish were of different kinds, about eight feet long, beautifully painted, and composed of transparent paper or silk. In some, the under jaw was made to move and the fins to wave, which appeared very natural. The Chinese are fond of show and harsh noise. but every face was cheerful, and much different from the gloomy solemnity of the church procession."*

CHAPTER VII.

TERMINATION OF THE EMBASSY—VOYAGE TO AND ARRIVAL IN INDIA.

On the 8th March, the Ambassador and suite got finally aboard the Lion and Hindostan, and at the same time Dr. Dinwiddie took up his berth in the Jackall, the vessel appointed for India. However, they were not yet to sail, and here, for several days, he was left in a position for serious reflection on the events of the last sixteen months. " Thus," he says, " the Embassy to me is ended. Its object was noble—the extension of commerce, and the improvement of science. With regard to the first, nothing that looks like an improvement has as yet taken place ; and as to the other object, little could be done in a country where, while at Pekin, we were prisoners, and on our journey

* Two Chinese, intending to become missionaries, were taken on board at Macao, and Dr. D. observes of them thus : " They go to Europe in the Hindostan, to the college Di Propagandi Fide. They speak only Chinese, and will pray with any book open very devoutly—a magazine, or any other, is all one. Why should England not have missionaries ? Those of other nations counteract her schemes."

hurried forward with hardly time to look at an object, and without being able to converse with the inhabitants. To travel through a fine country—to see pagodas, canals, and manufacturing towns, without being able to ask a single question, is extremely mortifying. To be conducted to the bottom of the Linho, by a Colao of the Empire—to receive a present from the Emperor at parting, and the Colao's farewell speech, without knowing a word he said, and consequently to fall into numberless blunders in our attempt to reply—what information could we derive respecting the arts and sciences in a country where we could not converse with the inhabitants? With what countenance will Lord Macartney return to Europe after his shameful treatment? No apology will satisfy. We go home—are asked what we have done. Our answer—we could not speak to the people."

Such was the termination of the Embassy. The philosopher, however, on leaving England, had firmly resolved not to return till he could extricate himself from embarrassment, and to try any part of the globe rather than plunge again into misfortune at home. His attention was now directed to the British empire in India, and to carry out his philosophical speculations there he had increased his apparatus largely by purchases from the Embassy, granted at prime cost. For upwards of a week the vessels were detained at the mouth of the harbor, awaiting the arrival of a fleet of Indiamen preparing for Europe under the protection of the Lion. While lying at anchor a singular circumstance occurred respecting the tides, which were so extremely irregular as to puzzle any theorist to account for the phenomena. "For a number of days the southerly wind has kept it constant flood; at least, if there is any ebb—it is more than overbalanced by the breeze, small though it sometimes be. We have been seven days at anchor, during which time the Lion has tended but once, and the Jackall not at all. The irregularity at Tonquin, mentioned in the Principia, does not, I believe, take place. Dr. Halley was misinformed by the pilots.

The Indiamen came dropping down the river till the 17th, when the whole fleet, amounting to eighteen vessels, took its departure, and the Embassy its final leave of the Celestial Empire.

The declaration of war between France and England had reached the gentlemen even at Pekin, and there it created among them considerable sensation, particularly in regard to the effect it might produce upon the Ambassador's movements. On their arrival at Canton they found the progress of the French arms exciting alarm, which rendered great precaution necessary for the safety of the fleet bound to Europe. The voyage, therefore, was one of peculiar interest. Every strange sail on the distant horizon was looked upon with suspicion, and gave rise to many a chase, though nothing occurred to cause any uneasiness. On the 29th March a Malay prow was seen ahead, and on the Jackall standing after her—she let go the long boat and took to her oars. The boat was picked up. Ten days after a fleet of these pirates, consisting of a square-rigged two-masted vessel, and about a dozen prows, were encountered near the island of Banca. These were chased by the Hindostan and Exeter, but nothing was elicited beyond the character of the chased. A boat, which was sent to the square-rigged vessel, found her almost deserted. Those remaining fell on their knees, but the crew of one of the prows behaved insolently, and drew their creses. They also refused to go to our Commander without orders from their own.

Upon April 14, the fleet for Europe came to anchor in the strait of Sunda, where it remained a few days before proceeding on the voyage, and where Dr. Dinwiddie was parted from his friends. The Jackall was now left with a squadron preparing for Bengal, under the protection of Commodore Mitchell, whose ship, the William Pitt, having sustained some damage was undergoing repairs. During this delay, it was arranged that the officers of the squadron, including Dr. Dinwiddie, should reside at the hotel in Batavia, where the Commodore's table was placed in the same room in which Lord Macartney's suite dined last year. When approaching the shore it was a fine Sunday morning, and the bell ringing for church elicited this remark : " It is a long time since we had any mark to distinguish Sunday from any other day in the week."

Batavia, as a commercial port, and as a place of rendezvous, is of great importance. It lies about a mile from the beach and is approached by a canal. A high square wall surrounds the city, and outside of this wall is a wide dirty ditch, or canal. The town is intersected by numerous canals, and emphatically is a " city of bridges," but presenting few public buildings interesting to a stranger beyond the citadel. St. Paul's church is, indeed, worthy of notice. Round the large dome of this edifice are the busts and escutcheons of all the governors of Batavia. The hotel, where every stranger *is obliged* to reside, is a very large and noble building. A high whimsical structure, called the observatory, contained not a single instrument of any kind, and the only memorial of what it has been—two stone pillars show where once a transit instrument had been mounted. A valuable collection of instruments, however, is said to have formerly belonged to this observatory.

" The town of Batavia may be looked upon as almost impregnable. The water is so shallow that no ship of war can come within gunshot of the works ; the place of landing is extremely difficult, while the works and canals could retard the progress of an army till it was cut off by the diseases of a country, perhaps the most unhealthy on the globe." " Through every part of the city the canals are extremely dirty, and mixed with all sorts of vegetable and animal matter. Sometime since, a proposal was made to cut down the trees from the streets, and to have some of the canals filled up ; but the inhabitants objected to the scheme on the ground that the trees existed in the days of their forefathers, and that it was wrong in the present government to pretend to be wiser than they were."

Outside the walls, an extensive suburb is chiefly inhabited by Chinese, apparently the most numerous, and evidently the most industrious people about all Batavia. Of Malays, another numerous race, many are held in bondage as slaves. This peculiar people was often the subject of conversation. Found in every country in the east, but inhabiting only the sea-boards, and distinct from the races of the interior, their origin is a source of great mystery. A savage expression of countenance and a thievish propensity rendered them often objects of much concern. Their insubordination was no less proverbial. The block-house, a square building near the hotel, mounting two guns with loop holes for musketry, once saved Batavia from an insurrection of this people.

The crese of the Malay is famous all over the east ; and it appears " he is sworn over one that has shed blood ; and the more it has shed the more solemn is the oath. Sometimes he is sworn over a gun barrel. A Malay never strikes with his crese direct, but inverted. In his handkerchief he carries a small weapon for cutting the throat. It is passed between the wind-pipe and neck, and the cut is made outwards. When two Malays fight a duel—the combatants seize each other by the hair, while they stab with the crese in the right hand. The matter is soon determined, and both generally are killed."

" The intrepidity of a savage may be gathered from his attachment to his arms. A Malay will as soon part with his life as his crese, and considers it an insult to be offered money for it, provided it has drawn blood. On the contrary, the Pelewese, an unwarlike people, readily part with their arms."

A greater contrast to the Malays than the Pelewese can scarcely exist among men. Captain Procter, on joining the Embassy, had just returned from Pelew, stored with anecdotes and observations confirmatory of the single-mindedness, hospitality, and good sense of the natives. Seeing the use of hair powder among the English, they asked— *Why do you wear powder ?* Because it is the fashion of our country. *Is it desirable to look old ?* was the innocent and earnest rejoinder.

Though much against the Doctor's will to be detained at Batavia, he found for a time his attention occupied with excursions along the shore, as well as to several of the channel islands. The indigo manufactures at Angeri Point, and the machinery at Onrust, are among the places referred to. Onrust, a fortified island in the roads of Batavia, is said to be the only safe place in the east for heaving down large ships. Sometimes these excursions were devoted to observations bearing on astronomy, geography, the climate, winds, and the tides, which latter had several peculiarities difficult of solution. The anchorage ground, along the Java shore, was so fast that sometimes the anchor could not be heaved, and the plan adopted was to set sail and drag the anchor ahead. An opportunity, too, was afforded of attending to the phenomena of earthquakes. About the middle of the second night at the hotel, our informant was roused by the first shock he ever felt, and he describes the sensation " like that of a strong man standing in the middle of a large room and, by the mere strength of his muscles, shaking the floor without leaping on it."

In regard to the celebrated poison tree, as described in the Philosophical Transactions, it is observed: " Its existence is absolutely denied at Batavia. Men have been sent on purpose to the spot where it was supposed to have grown, and no such tree could be found. On the contrary, at Bantam it was affirmed to be true, and that the king there keeps it a secret for the purpose of poisoning his arrows."

Among the feathered tribe, the maynoo bird was admired, and described as " somewhat less than a parrot, black, with a white spot near the tip of each wing, and a curious yellow ring round the neck, making an acute angle behind the apex, towards the head. Beneath the eyes are also two little curves. It is too delicate to live in Europe, but speaks better than the parrot, and can imitate the crying of a child, or the coughing of an old man."

A mode of catching monkeys is curious. " In a cocoa-nut, when emptied of its milk, a small hole is made, and the shell partly filled with sugar. The hole is of a size sufficient for the monkey to get in its hand, or fore foot, which, grasping a part of the sugar, is rendered too big to be withdrawn ; and such is the desire of the animal for the sugar that, rather than let go, it will suffer itself to be taken."

About Batavia the number of cocoa-nut trees is immense. They are from fifty to sixty feet high, straight and slender, with branches only at the top, where they spread out like the ribs of an umbrella. Under the branches, and near the centre, the nuts hang in clusters, five or six dozen on a tree, in different stages of ripeness. In order to reach the nuts, steps, or notches are cut into the tree. Many betel-nut trees are interspersed, straight and slender like the others, but neither so tall nor so strong. The betel-nuts grow in clusters like grapes.

In his excursions the Doctor was sometimes accompanied by the Commodore, who seemed too full of eccentricities for the important station which he held. After some observations on the heavenly bodies on Cooper's island, they started to return to Batavia, but greatly exceeded their calculations with regard to time, having lost their reckoning in the dark, and rowed for a full hour backwards. "The most able men are sometimes engaged in a frolic, but a man should have some ability to apologize for such follies, especially when he is Commander-in-Chief."

At the castle, one morning, an execution took place so early as six o'clock. " One man, a Chinese, was broken on the wheel, and a soldier, a European, beheaded. The scaffold consists of a square platform of brick raised about six feet above the level of the ground. On one side is a gallery with seats for the members of council, who attend. There were seven or eight gentlemen with red cushions before them. One read out of a book, which seemed a manuscript, for the space of more than half-an-hour; after which a clergyman prayed for about twenty minutes. The soldier was then instantly seized by two executioners, blindfolded by a black handkerchief, and conducted to the instrument, which consisted of two uprights, distant about fifteen inches, fastened by cross-pieces above and below; a frame, or block of wood, carrying an axe moved in grooves in the two uprights; a heavy lump of lead was fastened on the upper part of the axe-frame; to this was fixed a ring, and to the ring was tied one end of a piece of small cord, which went over a pulley, or through a hole on the top, and was brought down along one of the uprights, where it was fastened to a hook. The axe was of the common form, the edge a little curved, and about a foot in length along the edge. The criminal was placed on his knees on the inside, his head was then pulled by the hair down between the two uprights to a cross-piece, on which his throat was supported. With a chisel and mallet the cord, which suspended the axe, was cut at one blow, when the head was instantly severed from the body. The head was placed in front of the block, and the body was covered with a mat. All this was performed in less than one minute.

" The second criminal, who, at the separation of the other's head from the body, cried out, was immediately laid on the wheel, his arms and legs extended, and supported by wedges fixed in the frame, two to each leg, two to each thigh, and four to each arm. In this position he was tied fast to the frame by ropes. One of the executioners then took up a large iron crow, and, with one blow between each two wedges, broke the bones of his arms and legs—eight blows in all. He was now left on the wheel. About eight or ten other criminals were whipped, and most of them branded on the back with a hot iron. The mode of whipping was singular; two blows were given with *each* hand, one on the back, another on the ribs, with much dexterity.

"The wretch on the wheel was to receive the *coup de grace* at twelve o'clock—he was dead however before that time. The executioners went through their office without a single feeling in favor of the unhappy sufferers; and the spectators on the scaffold seemed equally unconcerned. Breaking the limbs on the wheel is the most shocking piece of barbarity that can be conceived. Is not death in its mildest form a sufficient punishment for any crime.?"

The Chinese were treated with much severity—they were forced to pay a dollar annually for liberty to wear the "pig-tail," or tuft of hair peculiar to themselves, besides a dollar for every child born, and another for every funeral, which is obliged to pass through a certain gate. "In short, the Dutch here take the same advantage that the mandarines do in China—they seize upon the Captain, as he is called, and make him answerable for the rest. In regard to the Malays—the Dutch affirm there would be no governing them without assuming a great deal of pomp and show; hence the origin and continuation of the stopping of carriages to members of the council, and some other customs, so much complained of by foreigners. There is more state, pride, and despotism here, than in any monarchy in Europe."

The Dutch authorities treated the officers of the squadron with perfect indifference; even Mr. Boswell, the English interpreter, was forbid assisting at the hotel. In regard to their walls and works they were almost as jealous as the Chinese, believing the English knew too much already. The consequence of this treatment was a burlesque on the stopping of coaches to *edile-heers*, or councilmen, played off by some officers of the squadron, assisted by some English residents. The cavalcade, which sallied twice forth at 4½ P.M. and again at six in the evening, afforded great amusement to the inhabitants. On the first occasion, "a major of the army, mistaking Spens for a real *edile-heer*, stopped, or rather his coachman stopped, his carriage. On discovering the mistake the major beat the coachman."

The delay at Batavia appeared to be most unnecessarily protracted.

" Our own coasts are deserted, our trade interrupted, while we are loitering here to please the Dutch." The repairs to the William Pitt exhibited gross mismanagement, and with a little care might have been completed in half the time. As an instance : after spending above six weeks, orders were given for several new sails under the excuse that those formerly received *got wet and rotted* on board the Canton. Disease was making sad havoc among both officers and men, and the apology for staying so long in such an unhealthy climate ought to have been a good one. " The climate is indeed the most serious consideration of all. The hands die, and I am afraid will die in great numbers before the arrival of the squadron in Bengal." Among other victims was Captain Cheap of the Nonsuch, who was buried with much respect in the Church-yard of Batavia, and at the request of the Commodore, an epitaph, in Latin, was composed for his tomb by Dr Dinwiddie.

"Europeans should never be employed in either wooding or watering in tropical climates ; their dress, also, should be altered. The tight bandages of the European dress is here extremely inconvenient ; and were this circumstance more attended to it would save the lives of numberless individuals who die under the *coup de soleil.*"

When preparations were at last made to go on board, the Dutch, who had treated the English with public contempt, now became anxious to prolong their stay. " An elegant gilded coach was sent by the General to the Commodore as a bribe to induce him to remain longer at Batavia, but this was rejected with becoming spirit—*It is now too late.* A message also declared that the Government did not know that the officers of the Bengal squadron lived at the hotel; but this insult, in the shape of an apology, was accepted in its true light." It was soon after given out that a French frigate was in the strait, and Government begged the assistance of an English ship to accompany the Dutch Commander in quest of the common enemy, while the other ships remained till their return. " All this was looked upon as a shallow artifice to induce a longer stay, but Commodore Mitchell, on this occasion, behaved with great propriety, and would not divide his squadron." Strange as it may seem ; even after all hands were aboard, beseeching letters, written in English, arrived to no better purpose. The die was cast, and the Dutch must now take care of themselves.

Towards the end of June the convoy left, and proceeded along the east coast of Sumatra in the direction of the strait of Banca, a channel full of islands, which rendered the navigation tedious and dangerous, and caused the anchor to be dropped several nights in succession. At day-light one morning, the Jackall had the misfortune to find the fleet entirely out of sight, without any information of the courses, or even places intended to call at. No rendevous whatever had been appointed in case of a separation. However, proceeding forward under all sail, some of the vessels hove in sight before it became dark. The strait of Dryan was found very inaccurate on the charts, many miles too far south, which was also the case with several islands. Some islands were not taken notice of at all, particularly a cluster of five little isles where a Malay prow escaped from the chase. This prow out-manœuvred its pursuers, and came to anchor under a rock, where the Nonsuch and Jackall fired a few shots to no purpose, being at too great a distance. The prow had the audacity to reply from a musket or swivel gun. Even after the ships had left it fired a few shots. The system of giving chase to every strange sail was rigorously carried out, but no Frenchman was discovered though his depredations were often heard of. Among the strangers encountered was one doubly strange, being no less than a Chinese junk navigating the ocean far from their usual tracks. It accompanied the squadron to the roads of Malacca, where the anchor was dropped on the 16th July. The Stromboli, of Bombay, was lying here greatly disfigured, having off Rajapore been struck with lightning, which splintered the topmast, shivered the topsail to ribbons, and killed four Europeans.

Here Dr. Dinwiddie went ashore immediately, and remained till late on the 19th, enjoying his several excursions, and speaking in flattering terms of the accommodation at the hotel, where he stayed.

" The town of Malacca is defended by a fort, consisting of a curtain and five small bastions, and is surrounded by a ditch. There are no works outside the walls beyond a sort of fluke, near the bastion at the north angle, containing embrasures for six cannons, but none mounted. It is extremely singular the Dutch should be so negligent in keeping their works in a proper state of defence. The works at Malacca are in the same condition, it is highly probable, in which they were received from the Portuguese."

A circumstance indicative of the early occupation of the settlement by Europeans appeared on some grave stones in the church-yard, which contained inscriptions one hundred and fifty years old.

Another unaccountable delay occurred here, during which a severe squall ensued for several days. In one instance the gale veered round the compass, driving some of the ships from their moorings. On the 27th, the voyage was resumed along the coast of Malacca, which according to the chart on board the Jackall (Sayer's) was laid down too much to the northward. The chase still continued to engross attention. When near Pulo Penang, an instance occured in which the chased turned out to be the Bombay frigate and Swift armed ship, proceeding to Malacca to take charge of a fleet of ten Indiamen going to China. No sooner was the character of the strangers ascertained than the chase dropped. They passed, however, without a single salute or compliment of any kind between the two Commanders. The Jackall desired to speak the frigate, but was vetoed. This vetoing the Jackall, and the coolness between the Commanders, seemed a strange state of things at such a critical period, when it was so essential to gain information, and be of service to each other. The Nautilus, however, one of the Bengal squadron, was immediately despatched to Pulo Penang for news, and returned to say that a French privateer had captured four English ships, two of which were lying at Penang ransomed. A signal was in consequence given for all captains to chase, but Dr. Dinwiddie wrote to the Commander insisting on the propriety of the Jackall proceeding immediately into the harbor, where she soon after came to anchor, while the rest of the fleet joined in pursuit of the French frigate of which intelligence had just been learned. The plants had suffered some damage from the heavy squalls, and it was feared the apparatus was in a bad condition. When brought ashore and examined, a part was much injured by dampness, but the glass was all safe.

At Batavia, the English squadron had been treated by the Dutch with contempt; at Pulo Penang it was very different—they were at home. Dr. Dinwiddie, who took up his residence with the Governor, Mr. Light, was received with the most marked attention, invited to his country residence, and escorted to all such objects as could be deemed interesting; while every information was afforded relative to the settlement, its people and productions. The settlement had existed for eight years, accompanied with this singular coincidence. " During the first four or five years there was much thunder and rain, and good crops. For the last two years there has been less thunder and rain, and bad crops. Fruit frequently now does not ripen, while a noxious air blows from the continent, and blasts whole trees. The water in the roads, too, from being very luminous formerly is now much less so."

Penang, otherwise called Prince of Wales Island, though an English settlement, was composed of people said to speak forty-eight different languages, twenty-seven of which were totally distinct. Chinese, widely scattered all over the east, formed a very important element in this population, and here their singular and industrious habits continued subjects of inquiry. " But," observes the Doctor, " employ a Chinaman by the day, and he will do nothing: let him have an interest in the business, and he will do everything."

Malays, too, with all their savage looks and piratical propensities, were, under the management of a kind Governor, no less industrious, and some of their operations were not only interesting but worthy of imitation. They could discover and separate brass filings from gold dust; could excel in the inlaying of gold; could temper iron by a process equal, if not superior, to Europeans; and could, when dyeing cloth blue, fix the color by a process which never fades. " In finding their way through the almost impenetrable forests of the torrid zone, they cut notches in the trees, and the son will frequently follow the steps of his father, and even grandfather."

In the gardens and plantations were cultivated most of the important vegetable productions of the east. Sago, bread-fruit, castor-nut, betel-nut, were abundant; pomegranates, guavas, mangoes, indigo, coffee-bean, pepper, cinnamon, &c. Among vegetables, the spontaneous production of the island, the elastic gum-tree became an object of some interest, and several young plants were added to the collection for the botanical gardens at Calcutta. This useful plant, from which the india-rubber is manufactured, was, as Dr. Dinwiddie observes, discovered in the woods by accidentally cutting one of the plants with a cutlass, when the milk drying it was found elastic. A plant called goatsfoot " is extremely useful in producing a soil on the driest and most barren sands." Another singular native is the *tawee-tawee* plant, which flies from tree to tree, seizing the upper part first, and descending in such a manner as always to kill the tree.

Some miles in the interior is an interesting waterfall, to visit which a whole day was devoted. Hard by, the Governor had a bungalo, where the party both breakfasted and dined. " The fall is upwards of 200 feet perpendicular, but is divided into different cascades. Above the principal one, the water runs under ground, where it is seemingly at a great depth, but sometimes a chink reveals it about 30 feet below. On either side a thick shade is formed by the trees, and there is little alteration in the quantity of water, which is cold and excellent. Sunshine on the falls looks beautiful."

" Governor Light has a snake twenty feet long, which he has kept about eleven months, and what is extraordinary, though victuals of different kinds have been thrown into the place, the snake has never been observed to eat, neither to drink. When touched with a stick, it rears its head from the middle of the coil in which it lies; and when gently rubbed seems pleased, as it raises up a whole coil." This reptile subsequently made its escape, swallowing a pig in its way. It was soon recaptured, but such was the feeble state of the digestive organs that it died with the load on its stomach.

On the return of the fleet, it appeared they had frequently chased but came up with nothing. The French privateer seemed to out-manœuvre our ships, as she still kept out of the way, and was only seen by merchantmen, several of which had been chased near this port. But if the mode of chasing was unfortunate that of giving signals was extremely so. Signals were frequently made when the topsail was directly between the flag and the ship to which it was directed. The parade, too, of unnecessary signals rendered the William Pitt more like a toy ship than the commander of a squadron. Sometimes the signal *to close* was read *to chase*, and all sail crowded. When last at anchor the signal *to close* was given before the signal to *weigh*. " The squadron, in short. exhibits striking proofs of want of ability, and consequently want of system."

Four weeks had elapsed since the Jackall anchored, and the squa-dron was once more in motion towards Bengal. A few days at sea, a large gray gull was observed astern, swimming after the vessel. In about a mile distance it came alongside and attempted to get up, in which it was assisted by one of the hands, and brought into the ship. " This is looked upon as an extraordinary circumstance, as these birds are very shy."

The manœuvres of Commodore Mitchell continued to be unac-countable. Another to the many instances of irregularity in the chase occurred in allowing a stranger to pass a long way to leeward, and what could have been effected in a quarter of an hour required by this procedure several hours. This part of the voyage proved more than usually disagreeable ; the squalls were excessive, and the sea rolled so grievously that the Nautilus, unable to contend with the swell, had to put back to Penang. The Jackall, being a small vessel, was ill calculated for such rough weather : it parted cable once and lost anchor, but was fortunately approaching Calcutta, where it arrived 27th September, 1794.

CHAPTER VIII.

RESIDENCE IN INDIA, AND APPOINTMENT AS PROFESSOR OF NATURAL PHILOSOPHY IN THE COLLEGE OF FORT WILLIAM.

IMMEDIATELY on landing Dr. Dinwiddie delivered the despatches, and on the 30th, at the levee, was introduced to Sir John Shore, the Governor-General, who was particularly curious about the Chinese mission. For this purpose the Doctor was invited to dine with His

Excellency on the following day; it also afforded an opportunity of talking over the state of business in India. By this time, he had delivered his letters of introduction, and was altogether pleased with his prospects. He was, however, landed in what was considered the most expensive city in the world, and where every exertion he could put forth would be requisite to gain success. His letters proved of great service, and, receiving ample encouragement, he lost no time in preparing, under the patronage of His Excellency, the Governor-General, for a course of lectures in experimental philosophy, which at once established his fame and independence in Bengal. To use his own words:—" My success at Canton enabled me to procure a credit on Calcutta for a small sum sufficient to set matters afloat. 1 opened a subscription, and in the course of a few weeks had the plea-sure of delivering my introductory lecture to a company of one hundred and eighty of the first ladies and gentlemen in the settle-ment. The subscription was one hundred rupees, which, if remitted to England, at the present rate of exchange, would amount to £2,250, the greatest sum that, probably, ever was received for one course in any part of the world."

Thus, in Calcutta, was Dr. Dinwiddie established as a lecturer on natural philosophy and chemistry, but he did not confine himself to these subjects alone, his next course being the antient and modern art of war. Private instructions, too, in the various branches of science and art formed part of his arrangements here, as formerly in Europe. His knowledge of applying theory to practice suggested to the Board of Trade the idea which shortly procured an appointment in the service of the East India Company. The nature of these services will be better comprehended from the following official docu-ment recommending the engagement :—

To the Honourable Sir John Shore, Bart.,
Governor General in Council,
Fort William.

Board of Trade.

HONOURABLE SIR,—We beg to represent to your Honourable Board that we have frequently wished to consult Dr. Dinwiddie in several parts of chemistry, mechanics, and natural philosophy, which have relation to the affairs under our charge, and by which possible improvement beneficial in its consequences to the country and the Company might be obtained. But we have been withheld from making any references to him by our inability to make him any recompence. We have no cause to think that he would not readily gratuitously attend to any application from us. But we cannot in reason ask him to impart his knowledge, the result of many years study and observation, and which is now his profession, without having it in our power to render a due return.

2. The particular matters on which we wish to advise with him are as fol-low :—

IN CHEMISTRY.

The modes of bleaching in Europe, as improved within these last few years, compared with the modes long used in this country. It is possible the former may be introduced with great advantage both in respect to expedition, to the preservation of the quality of the cloth, and to a decrease of expense. The subject is worth inquiry.

IN MECHANICS.

The defective powers of the sugar mills used by the natives we believe injure the preparation of the juice: The rivers of this country are unfavorable to mill work: The cattle are weak and expensive: And the only windmill that has been constructed has failed, owing, as we understand, to the frequent hard gales, and long continued calms that are so prevalent in these provinces. Probably the improved steam engine might be found to answer as a power for mill work for sugar, and eventually for other purposes.

NATURAL HISTORY.

The Court of Directors are earnest in their wishes that the raw silk of Bengal should be improved, so as to render an importation into Great Britain from China and Italy unnecessary. Our endeavours will be strenuously given to forward so desirable an object But in the event of its failing it would be well to ascertain whether physical causes, or want of skill in the preparation, oppose success.

3. These are the points which at present occur to us: Others may arise. But we wish it to be understood that we consider our views as speculative; as matters rather worthy of research and inquiry than as at present promising success. Though, if successful, it is impossible to say what future benefits may arise therefrom, while the expense attending the research cannot be considerable. Dr. Dinwiddie's knowledge need not be confined solely to our inquiries; but he might be requested to extend his advice to any subjects that should be referred to him from any other department; and to communicate any observations on manufactures, chemistry or science, that might be useful in promoting the prosperity of the Company's provinces.

4. If our ideas meet the approbation of your Honourable Board, we submit to you the making him such compensation as may seem proper to give: and we have the less hesitation in referring our suggestions to you, as " the Company have never been deterred by the want of a spirit of enterprise, and still less by a false principle of economy, from using every endeavour to extend the trade and to cultivate knowledge and science in every way that might prove beneficial to the British Empire."

" We are, &c.,

Fort William, the 16 June, 1795.	(Signed)	JOHN BRISTOW. JOHN HALDANE. RICHARD KENNAWAY. JOHN BIBB."

This arrangement laid open a wide field for the Doctor's research. Among other experiments, we find him testing and reporting on the qualities of indigo, cochineal, saltpetre, gunpowder, flax and hemp, and the native timbers of the country, in regard to the purposes of architecture and ship-building. We find him also attending to the erection of lightning-rods, the management of fire-engines, pumps; to regulating chronometers, and a variety of other matters. In short,

H 2

he was as busy as his situation would permit in collecting curious
and useful information; in attending all the processes of the natives
in refining of gold and silver, in which they excel; spinning, weaving, bleaching, dyeing, &c., their different cloths; with every other
art or manufacture he could hear of. "A habit," says he, "of examining manufactures for twenty years past at home has given me
much experience; and the possession of a large apparatus enables me
to perform every experiment." Not only the Board of Trade, but
the Medical, Marine, and Military Boards, occasionally consulted him
on subjects connected with their departments. At the termination
of these services, in 1797, Government was pleased to express its
approbation of the manner in which they had been discharged.

Unconnected with his obligations to the Company, he was at the
same time engaged in experiments of a nature too extensive for, and
altogether unsuited to, a lecture-room. Among other articles of
European importation, difficult of access, was vitriolic acid, the high
price of which had hitherto been a great drawback to the indigo and
other manufactures; but by his suggestion, and under his management, works were constructed by which it could be obtained at one
quarter the usual Bengal price. This was followed up, but on a
much smaller scale, with other acids, particularly nitric acid, which
became extensively applied to medical purposes with success. The
Dispensary, anxious for this article in its most genuine state, was
supplied by contract from the Doctor's private room.*

Neither did his official duties interfere with his professional engagements as a public lecturer, nor restrict his operations to any particular locality. His success in the City of Palaces encouraged him
in an adventure upon Madras, which could be easily reached by sea,
and where he landed soon after the commencement of 1796. The
Governor, Lord Hobart, approved of his views, and cheerfully became
his patron. Dr. Dinwiddie had already met with several of his

---

* That the genuine article was at a premium may easily be inferred from
the following extract of a letter sent by Dr. D. to his agent in London: "I
was not a little surprised, a few days ago, on trying the specific gravity of the
London nitric acid, to find the result *not quite eleven*. In short, on farther
examination, I found that the bottle had been filled, at least three-fourths of
the whole contents, with water. This must have been done at the works, for
it had not been opened here, nor do I suppose you opened any of them.
These pitiful advantages taken by British manufacturers, particularly in
articles sent to this country, will ultimately recoil on themselves. The
abominable trash poured into this country, by every ship from Europe, under
the name of hats, boots, shoes, telescopes, with a long *et cetera*, tend greatly to
accelerate the establishment and progress of manufactures in India. The
cockney phrase—My dear sir, this here hat is not for sale—it is for the Ingee
market—is well known here."

European audience occupying important positions in society, and it turned out that His Excellency, and Admiral Sir E. K. Elphinstone, then at Madras, and a subscriber on this occasion, had both, unknown to the Doctor, attended his lectures in Europe, the former in Dublin, and the latter in London. His Lordship embraced the opportunity to have a number of articles tested by the apparatus, particularly the manufacture of saltpetre and gunpowder, respecting which a number of experiments were tried and reported on.

The system of education—for which Dr. Bell of Madras became afterwards celebrated—was just beginning to attract public attention. It wrought successfully in the schools attached to the observatory here, where the boys were educated as surveyors and engineers. Dr. Dinwiddie, who was invited to an examination of the system, observes, "Landscape, architecture, and surveys, are drawn extremely well. The two schools prove that the opinion, generally maintained in Bengal, that the country born are inferior in mental acquirements to Europeans is unfounded. I never saw, in any school in Britain, such proficiency, by boys so young, in almost every branch of education."

During this period, two Cingalese Ambassadors arrived at Madras on some mission to Lord Hobart, and, for their entertainment, a number of experiments were performed by the express desire of His Excellency. The apparatus was fitted up in the Exchange-rooms, which had been kindly granted by the committee for the purpose of the lectures. On the walls were the portraits of Lord Cornwallis and General Dundas, which the Cingalese strangers observing, inquired who they were. From the proximity of Ceylon, it was fancied the names of the generals would be well known to the Cingalese. But the English were astonished to learn that these strangers had never heard of either the name of Cornwallis or Dundas, nor of Hyder Ally, nor of the horrible wars which had reduced so large a portion of the peninsula to a desolate waste. The Dutch, who occupied the whole seacoast of their country, had so effectually shut the Cingalese out from the world as to keep them in utter ignorance of all that was passing around.

An absence of four months restored the Doctor to Calcutta, where, at proper intervals, he continued, under the patronge of the Marquis Wellesley, who had succeeded to the reins of government, to deliver those lectures, which had been so auspiciously begun. The subscription list did not always come up to the proper mark, but nevertheless neither did it fall so low as to discourage him in his profession. Independent of a large library, and a fine collection of antiquities, curiosities, shells, minerals, and models, his philosophical apparatus

alone was valued at twenty thousand rupees. His travels had
furnished him with much new information, which was embodied in
the lectures as circumstances favored. The course on China was,
indeed, laid aside, but illustrations from that country were often introduced, and the progress of art and science there frequently contrasted with that of other nations, both antient and modern. "The
first missionaries," says he, "found China, when compared to Europe,
superior in many respects ; but Europe has improved so much within
these two centuries, that the comparison is now totally different."
The progress of science in Europe had indeed been and was now
astonishing, and it was watched with an anxious eye. Every important improvement or discovery was hailed with the feelings of a
decided votary. Extensive commissions of books and apparatus were
yearly remitted to his orders in Bengal. The many applications for
books and apparatus to be sent, through his agency, into all parts of
India, proved the spirit of inquiry which he had diffused around.
Good articles were difficult of access, and much reliance was placed
on the experience of Dr. Dinwiddie, who became, in a manner, the
centre or focus of philosophy in the East. His correspondence
was very extensive, and bears ample testimony to his zeal, in promoting researches in every branch of science, and the assistance he lent
to those desirous of acquiring information on subjects connected with
it. Astronomical and meteorological observations, governmental
surveys, minerological discoveries, and discoveries made in translating
antient Hindoo manuscripts, formed interesting features in his correspondence, which was sometimes carried on in the Latin and French
languages. Except the temporary voyage to Madras, he never left
the vicinity in which he first established himself. Frequent appeals
had been made to visit other extensive and remote towns, but engagements at head-quarters, combined with the difficulty of transporting
the apparatus, seem to have been the main obstacles to a desire he
had often cherished.

Soon after settling in Calcutta, he was elected a member of the
Asiatic Society, founded by Sir William Jones for investigating the
arts, sciences, and antiquities of Asia. The society then stood upon
a very unsatisfactory foundation—without a place to meet in—without a library or museum ; but what was considered a greater desideratum—without a committee to investigate the merits of the
different papers communicated for publication in their *transactions*.
The secretary, on whose shoulders most of the business devolved, was
in the habit of carrying the communications about for the opinions
of such members as he thought proper to consult. Through the
exertions of Dr. Dinwiddie, a meeting was called to take these and

other matters into consideration; but, unfortunately, before the appointed day, he met with a serious accident from breaking a bottle of vitriolic acid, which confined him for upwards of a week, and prevented his attendance. The annexed letter to the President had some influence in laying the basis on which the institution afterwards stood :—

August 19th, 1796.

SIR,—As the Asiatic Society meet this evening for the special purpose of considering the best means of rendering the institution permanent, and of determining whether a house should be provided for their future meetings, permit me to offer a few observations, which indisposition prevents me from making in the society, itself.

The following regulations would, in my opinion, tend to improve and render permanent the society :—

Regulation 1st—Stated and regular meetings, once in the month at least; once in the week would probably be better.

Objection 1st.—The President cannot possibly attend so often. *Answer*—Choose two or more Vice-Presidents.

Objection 2nd.—We shall sometimes want papers. *Answer*—When that happens to be the case spend the time in conversing on useful subjects. At a conversation, as it is called, of this sort, held at Sir Joseph Banks's, in London, more information may be obtained in two hours than in many months' reading and study.

Regulation 2nd.—A Committee to select papers and superintend the publication of the *Asiatic Researches*. The Transactions of the Royal Society of London were, for many years, under the sole direction of the secretary. Complaint, however, of supposed partiality became so frequent as to induce the society to elect a committee for the above purpose. The old adage may, I hope without offence, be applied to the secretary of any society, or to any man whatever, *pro omnia possumus omnis*. To this it may be replied, the secretary can consult some of the members individually respecting the merits of a paper. I answer—To hack about and expose, much more to write answers and comments on a paper, which has not as yet been read, is as disrespectful to the society as to the author.

Regulation 3rd.—A Library and Museum are desirable objects, and what would tend to render the institution permanent. The principal obstacles at present to these and to a house seem to be the smallness of the number of members, and fluctuation of the society.

I should have troubled the society with a few more hints drawn from experience, but that the hopes of being able to attend have induced me to postpone writing this till too late.

I am, &c.,

J. DINWIDDIE.

HON. SIR JOHN SHORE, Bart.,
President of the Asiatic Society.

The first two regulations were adopted, and the other reserved for future consideration. At the first weekly meeting the Doctor was chosen one of the committee of papers, on which he continued during his residence in India. By his advice, at an early meeting, the society also adopted a resolution of publishing their transactions (the Researches) at their own expense.

When Dr. Dinwiddie arrived in India, science was much neglected, or at best confined to few hands. Mathematics was at a low ebb, even among the officers of the British army, which was often the subject of regret to some honorable exceptions to the general rule. A few years had but elapsed since Lord Cornwallis laid siege to Bangalore, when, most shameful to relate, not one man among the engineers could measure the distance of the enemy's works. It was determined to be twelve hundred yards, but when the battery began to play the guns could not reach the works. In this dilemma, Colonel Ross was sent for, from Madras, on purpose to determine the distance, which was found to be two thousand yards. In several instances, officers, entrusted with a governmental survey, found the lecture-room useful in getting their mathematics brightened up for the field. For the first few years, the best mathematician met with was a native of the name of Tuffus-ul-Husien, afterwards Prime Minister to the Nabob of Oude; but his knowledge was purely speculative, being unable to apply it to any practical purpose. He was highly delighted with the Doctor's acquaintance, and became a regular attendant for some years. Another native pupil of distinction was Hurry Mohun, the author of several learned translations.

The lecture-room was occasionally visited by the Brahmins, among whom the Doctor's astronomical reputation gained much influence by essential service rendered in the case of an eclipse of the moon. The Brahmins were divided in opinion whether the luminary would rise before or after the beginning of the eclipse. It was a matter of great consequence for them to know, as the ceremonies attendant upon the occasion were quite different in the two cases. In this dilemma, application was made to the Doctor, who informed them that the moon would rise eclipsed, about twenty minutes after the beginning, as the event proved.

His celebrity among distinguished natives had extended even to a great distance, as appears from the following singular circumstance. One day he was waited upon by two native strangers come on a mission from the Rajah of Nepaul. It appeared that the Rajah had heard that Dr. Dinwiddie maintained that the earth turned round once in twenty-four hours, and, being puzzled to account for it, had sent his vakeel all the way to Calcutta on purpose to ascertain how this happened. The Doctor, who was highly amused at the mission, kindly appointed the next day to elucidate the mystery. He was indeed busy at the time with some experiments on indigo, but these were laid aside to gratify the curiosity of the strangers by a lecture

on the orrery, not only explaining the annual and diurnal revolutions
of the earth but also other astronomical phenomena, with which they
departed highly satisfied.

But little encouragement was nevertheless received from the natives. " Nothing will prevail on a native to part with his money for
instruction. He is liberal only in nautches and ridiculous ceremonies.
A native, who will sometimes lay out half a lac on a festival, will
grudge to pay a gold mohur per month for his son at school. Though
rich, he will live in a house dirty and mean beyond the conception of
a European. There is not perhaps any circumstance in which the
Asiatics differ more from the Europeans than in their houses, furniture, and mode of living. They are so fond of lawsuits and wrangling that, if a father leaves property at his death, the sons seldom
abide by his will, but instantly go to law, and continue the litigation
till the subject of contention is consumed."

The character of the Hindoos seems to have been an object of considerable interest to the Doctor, who, from his own experience, further
informs us : " The arts of flattery and dissimulation are practised with
considerable address. I received a visit from Gopee and Hurry
Mohun. The former asked me, whether there was any other in
England as learned as I am ! In making this compliment, it was to
borrow a telescope to observe the transit of Mercury. Divination
and witchcraft infect all classes from the highest to the lowest in the
land. Hurry Mohun believes in palmistry, the rules of which he
knows, and tried them on my hand. When told that such predictions sometimes failed, his answer was ready—*an error in the calcula-
tion.* This is like want of faith when a miracle is attempted without
success. When anything about the house is lost, or mislaid, as
sometimes happens, and a native and a European are searching at the
same time—if the former finds it, he says, *my God showed me to it.*
Perjury among Hindoos is nothing thought of. For a month's
wages, a witness may be procured to swear to anything. A man
wanted to arrest his neighbour for taking 10,000 fish out of his pond.
A witness was found, and *this number actually sworn to*, and valued
at 6,000 rupees. When a quarrel or misunderstanding takes place
between two natives, it is seldom forgotten, and here, as in more
civilized countries, is sometimes decided by a duel. In one instance,
matchlocks were used ; each applying the muzzle to his antagonists
breast. On a signal given they fired ; one, however, hung fire, while
the other shot his antagonist through the heart. In the law courts,
Mussulmen are sworn on the Koran—Hindoos on the water of the
Ganges, which is considered as a sacred oath, unless they can find
means of muddying or rendering the water impure. In this case the
oath is not binding. But their most solemn oath is with the hand on

a cow.   A native under sentence of death, being desirous of having
his will made, requested the attendance of Mr. M‘Nabb, attorney, to
whom he wrote a letter, which began thus:—*Sir, as I am to be hanged
to-morrow, &c.*"

"Information received from the pundits is not always to be
depended on.   They endeavor to conceal everything that tends to
expose the ignorance or wickedness of their writers, or that seems to
discountenance any of their present dogmas.   They carefully conceal
or alter many passages in their antient and as they call them sacred
writings.   Lieutenant Wilford informs me that Hindoo books seldom
last forty years, the paper decays, and is corroded by worms.   The
consequence is, books have frequently to be reproduced.   In doing
this, the pundits generally introduce something of their own.   No
traces of dialling have been found among the Hindoo writers.   Lieutenant W. has, however, taught his pundit, some of the European
methods of drawing dials, which he, the pundit, it is believed, will
introduce into some work he may be employed in copying; and sixty
or hundred years hence, it may be considered as the *antient Hindoo
mode of making dials*.   This is extremely probable, seeing that Mr.
Davis has discovered *Charles' Oak* in the antient Hindoo map of the
heavens."

"Scientifically, there are many striking omissions in the Hindoo
books.   The Governor-General has one of the most learned pundits
in the country.   This gentleman in a conversation with the vakeel,
my pupil, told him (the v.) that there was nothing in the Sanscrit
books on the subject of mechanics; and he (the pundit) denied the
possibility of performing by human labor what Europeans related to
be the effect of mechanism."

"To calculate an eclipse is the summit of every Hindoo's wish in
the astronomical line.   In their computations these astronomers use
things instead of numbers.   When they desire any number to be
doubled or multiplied by two—they say *by hand* or *feet*, there being
two of each.   When tripled—they say *by fire*, alleging there are *three*
kinds of fire.   Multiplied by four—they use *vedas*, the number of
these books being *four*.   By five—*fingers* are employed; and so on."

"The knowledge and skill of the natives are best seen in useful and
ingenious arts, some of which are carried to great perfection, and
among others that of spinning is remarkable.   It is performed by the
hand alone without the aid of a wheel.   To such an extraordinary
degree of fineness are the threads sometimes drawn out that the
spinner cannot see them without the aid of a vessel of water, in which
the shadow is reflected.   The cloth made from this thread was bought
up by princes and great men; little, however, is now spun so fine."

With so much skill and ingenuity it is curious that instances of unaccountable ignorance is met with. " Coal has been found by Mr. Elliot to the eastward, where the natives have, from time immemorial, been accustomed to extract an oil from it. This oil they apply in cutaneous cases, but till shown by Mr. E. they had never used coal for fuel."

Speaking of agriculture, we learn " a Mr. Mallet has arrived with machinery in the agricultural line, and talks of introducing great improvements. He means to plough deep furrows with an English plough drawn by two horses. This gentleman has not considered the business well. A native plough costs but a few annas; the ploughman can carry it on his shoulder to and from the field, while deep ploughing would be an injury to the crop. The soil for rice is simply scratched. The ryot, or Bengal farmer, will not only carry his plough on one shoulder, but will take the harrow and other implements on the other shoulder. Even the corn is all carried home on the head, no hackerries being ever used."

"As a general rule, poor people seem happier and richer than the same class in Europe. They have nose-rings and other ornaments, generally of gold, and they want neither houses, clothes, nor fuel, three most expensive articles in colder climates. A very little, too, is necessary to support life. A man who attended Mr. S.'s sheep and poultry for two years received only one rupee, eight annas (about 3s. 9d.) a month, yet he had a wife and six children to support on that sum."

" In a commercial point of view there is some probability of the natives supplanting Europeans, numbers of whom are continually entering the service of princes, and introducing European knowledge, which is gradually taking root. All the arts and manufactures will, no doubt, in time be practised by the natives, who, from their mode of living, will always undersell a European. They can now make as good indigo at one-half the expense. Twenty years ago, a European tailor charged 120 to 130 rupees for a coat, now about one-half, while a native tailor will furnish as good an article for one-half of that, or 30 rupees."

Lying and cheating are vices not confined to any class, neither is it considered a crime if they are exercised on Europeans. Even when the person does not expect to be believed, he still persists in his story, which, being previously contrived for the purpose, he is determined not to lose the benefit of. As an instance out of many, the sirdar bearer was detected thieving some silvered speculums and other articles from the lecture-room, yet such was the impudence of the fellow that he persisted in denying though several of the articles were found in his possession. Even after being turned away, he again protested his innocence, and made earnest appeals to be re-instated in his office. The electrical machine, however, on one or two occasions, was found to be possessed of a virtue too powerful for such pertinacity. A gentleman suspected his servant of embezzling certain sums of money, which the latter denied in spite of a severe flogging. It was arranged to bring the culprit before the machine when he was told what would be the consequence if he was guilty; but the fellow still persisted in his innocence. The jar had been previously charged, and when asked to touch it—such was the effect of the shock that he instantly fell down; but soon after got upon his knees, and, in an imploring attitude, confessed everything.

As a curious contrast to this inflexible obstinancy of a Hindoo may be mentioned the case of a Mussulman, who was in the service of the Doctor, as darwan, or porter. " This man was detected in secreting some phials and other articles from the chests last brought from the custom-house; in consequence, I turned him off. The moment he was charged with the crime he confessed, but seemed very little affected at the discovery."

On another occasion, however, a strange act of honesty is recorded. Every inhabitant of any consequence always goes a visiting in his palanquin, attended by bearers, &c. Returning from the country one evening in the dark, the lantern-bearer came into contact with a hackerry, and smashed the lantern to pieces. On getting up early the next morning, we read " I was surprised to find a bullock in my compound. On inquiry I learned it was put there by the lantern-bearer as security for the price of the lantern smashed last night."

" With all their knavery, and all their religious prejudices, the lower classes in Bengal are much more polite than in Europe. The man employed in keeping my apparatus clean never begins work till he has made his salaam to me, and for this purpose he comes to me in whatever room of the house I may be, or at whatever distance from the place in which he works. It is the same with all other workmen."

The religious prejudices of the Hindoos are most extraordinary, and a continual annoyance to Europeans, as they will not handle anything that has touched flesh, liquor, &c. The sirdar-bearer already alluded to was once with difficulty obliged to take some drinking glasses from the lecture room, and carry them up stairs. Immediately after he washed himself all over. On a table, where a piece of flesh had been placed, some silver money was laid down for this same individual, but rather than lift it himself, he went to the other side of the street and brought a Mahometan to put it into his hands. To a Hindoo an eclipse is always an important event, and once when the moon was, or about to be, in this interesting way, Dr. Dinwiddie had occasion for his hair-dresser, and sent for him, but he refused to come till the eclipse was over. " The man who attends to my apparatus also observed—We are all ordered to pray for the moon." As a specimen of religious folly, it would be difficult to surpass this. " If you go into a Hindoo house, while the family is at dinner, not only the victuals, but the dishes are thrown away." Annoying or foolish as these absurdities are, they become trifling when compared to an unhappy circumstance, in which a fire consumed a woman, a child, and a cow. Strange as it may seem, the Hindoos lamented the death of the cow more than the woman and child. But even this again is outdone. " A poor man, whose home was lately burned, had a cow burned to death at the same time. For this loss to himself, the unfortunate man is condemned by the Brahmins to walk through the streets for one year, bellowing like a cow. He passed where I was this morning (June 29, 1796) bellowing for certain like the animal for the death of which he suffers."

" Some writers who have only been a year or two in India have described the Hindoos as an innocent people, and have given them courage, honesty, and so forth. But these writers have never been able to converse with the inhabitants. The real character of the lower orders of Hindoos can be learned only from housekeepers long resident in the country, and having transactions with them. It has been alleged in support of their courage that a Hindoo has plunged his knife into his bosom rather than submit to what he considered an indignity. But the behaviour of the Hindoo arose from the desire of revenge, as he believes his ghost will perpetually torment those who occasioned his death."*

" The splendour of the Bengal Government," we are told, " was much diminished by Lord Cornwallis, and in consequence the English character lowered in the estimation of the natives, who take many liberties with Europeans. Natives, however, are not admitted to any share in the government. Neither are they into places of trust, or emolument, not even into the company of Europeans. Sir J. Murray is said to be the almost only English gentleman in the settlement who entertains the natives in his own house, and enters into their affairs,

* A tolerably numerous class about Calcutta are native Portuguese, from whom Dr. D. received many applications for employment. " Most of the native Portuguese," he observes, " are in a poor and wretched state, and the lower orders of them are said to be more deficient in morality than either the Hindoos or Mussulmen. It is very remarkable that these Indian Portuguese are, in general, of a darker complexion than either of the other two sections. Does this not prove that climate exercises an important influence on color?"

amusements, &c. The son of a rajah is here in a state of indigence, although his father, at the taking of Calcutta by Sijah Dowlah, was the best friend the English had. Sir J. Shore refuses the son an audience. The order of the Court of Directors will not even admit of boys born of country mothers, which puts the boys in a very awkward predicament. The increase of these half-breeds, otherwise called *country-born*, is so rapid that in time some great change must take place."

" Native princes keep introducing the military discipline of Europe. Their battalions are now well managed, and the day will probably come when some prince of more than ordinary ability will have the address to unite the different native powers and expel the Europeans from the country. The regularity of the pay in the Company's service is the best guarantee for the fidelity of their battalions ; while the native princes are always much in arrear with their armies. Another wise precaution in the Company's service is—half the Sepoys in every native regiment are Mussulmen—the other half Hindoos. These opposite prejudices prevent a union, or conspiracy against the officers."

In some respects, however, the Government is often and justly censured. For instance : " It seems extraordinary that the Court of Directors should permit foreigners to trade with India, and yet persist in refusing that privilege to the British. London might be made the emporium of Indian commodities. The number of foreign ships now trading to India supply foreign markets with those articles which they would be obliged to procure through the medium of British navigation. The impolicy appears evident. What reasons, then, do the Court of Directors give for their conduct in this matter. ?"

Dr. Dinwiddie always took a lively interest in the war which continued between England and France, and he writes thus on October 5, 1798, at 2¼ P.M. : " By an overland express, I have this moment learned that England is invaded,—the floating batteries evaded our fleet, which was prevented from coming up with them by a current. Though at 10,000 miles distance, what awful scenes suggest themselves ! England at this moment under the dominion of France ! It cannot be ! Not a true Briton but will sooner die than become a slave. What anxiety to learn particulars !"

On this head, satisfactory particulars very soon arrived, but the destruction to English shipping in the Indian Ocean continued a sad subject of complaint ; and he breaks out in the following strain when the news arrived of a fresh capture. " What a disgrace to have our ports insulted by a petty privateer, while such a naval force is lying *idle* in the harbour ? Where is the Nonsuch, a vessel armed by this Government expressly for the purpose of protecting our trade ? We order matters prettily enough, and they will never be properly conducted in this country till there shall be but one supreme power, the King, or the Company. Both occasion so many contrary interests— so much clashing of power—that the public service is greatly hurt by it. A King's ship, being independent of the Governor in Council, may refuse any service it is sent on."*

The latter years of the 18th century gave rise to a controversy which elicited a deal of interest among learned and curious individuals. This controversy, which originated in private conversation in the Doctor's presence, was no less than the year on which the 18th century would terminate—1799, or 1800. To ordinary intelligible minds the question seems simple enough ; nevertheless, a heavy wager was the consequence, the money was staked, and great exertions used to bring forward authorities on the matter. The question was not only discussed in the papers, but it became the subject of a lecture, which showed that two modes, named the *cardinal* and *ordinal*, had been adopted in reckoning centuries ; and that—if the question was to be decided by *authority*—it would be in favor of the *cardinal* mode, which would terminate the century with the last day of 1799. Such was the view which the Doctor took of the question, because independent of the most learned authorities, it was supported by Act of Parliament. But, as there were also learned authorities on the other side, a drawn battle was eventually agreed to in regard to the stakes—none of the combatants, however, being converted. In practice, the *cardinal* undoubtedly had the advantage, but certainly not in theory. A few learned men may have studied this question ; it is, nevertheless, far from being generally known that two modes of terminating the century have prevailed, which cannot be a matter of opinion, and consequently absurd. Common sense tells any man who can reason that 100, or 1800 years, will only be completed on the last days respectively of those years. If then a century means

---

* During the war, a very affecting episode is related by Dr. D. of one of his friends, a military captain, named Davis, who took a peculiar fancy to see a naval fight. Accustomed as he had been to the horrors of a battle on land he yet sighed to witness the sickening scene at sea, and for this purpose went a volunteer on board the Sybelle frigate, Capt. Cooke, in search of the French frigate La Forte, which was committing great havoc among British shipping at the very port of Calcutta. The enemy was found just as the shades of even descended, and was captured after an obstinate resistance of one hour and forty minutes. The Sybelle suffered little, having only 3 or 4 men killed ; among them, nevertheless, was Capt. Davis, who fell at the very commencement of the action.

a 100 years—how comes such men as Gibbon, Robertson, Lalande, Playfair, and numerous others, not to speak of the Act of Parliament, nor book of Common Prayer, to have acquiesced in the *cardinal* mode of terminating the century, or in 1799 ?

At the close of the century Dr. Dinwiddie's prospects were not so flattering, and he first began seriously to think of returning to Europe. He then entertained the idea of an overland journey in order to visit the classic regions of Egypt, Palestine, Greece, and Italy. The particulars of his travels were arranged, and the only hinderance to his departure was the apparatus, which now hung upon him like an incubus, and chained him to the spot. He tried in vain to dispose of it by lottery ; even a portion of it would not raise the requisite number of subscribers. The spirit for improvement, and even the taste for rational amusement, seems now to have been quite lost in Calcutta. A course of lectures had to be given up after the third evening for want of a sufficient audience. Unwilling however to remain idle, he formed a partnership to become brewer and distiller, and gave up all further intention of lecturing again. " It is extremely provoking to a man of science to relinquish his favorite studies for want of encouragement ; " at least, such were the Doctor's feelings when packing up the apparatus to be laid aside as useless. Extensive premises were engaged at Tangrah, a few miles in the country, where the business was to be carried on, and where the Doctor also fixed his residence to look after the works. But this speculation was attended with many unforeseen difficulties and proved quite unfortunate. It was entirely new, and every requisite had to be provided. The burden rested mainly on the Doctor's shoulders ; and before he resigned his interest in the concern, he had much reason to regret his connexion with it. In the meantime a more honorable employment, and one more congenial to his feelings, awaited him at Fort William, where he was appointed to a Professor's chair in the newly instituted college. This was looked upon as a happy turn in his affairs, as there was now a prospect of making something of the apparatus, which was again to be brought into activity. When known for certain that the college would be proceeded with, books and instruments rose to an immoderate price, and the Doctor, who, but a few months before, would have disposed of any article at less than prime cost, would not now sell at any price, though he had many offers. He even began to add to his collection under the impression that Government would, in the end, purchase the whole for the use of the college.

When the college went into operation, Dr. Dinwiddie entered upon his duties as Professor of Mathematics, and also of Natural Philosophy and Chemistry. The arrangement of the mathematical classes, and the analysis of the lectures, were first submitted and approved of by the College Council, who ordered the latter to be printed for the use of the students. The lectures consisted of alternate courses on natural philosophy and chemistry, with two courses occasionally between on some branch of natural history, and the antient and modern art of war. Public lectures also were resumed as circumstances favored, and the new science of galvanism proved both acceptable to the audience and advantageous to himself. It created a deal of interest throughout India at this period, particularly in its application to medical purposes. The Doctor was successful in drawing the attention of the profession to this important discovery, from a number of cures effected by himself, and in particular a singular case of chorea, or dance of St. Vitus, which was attended with some remarkable circumstances. The following letter, published in the *Calcutta Gazette*, fully explains the interest taken in this subject:—

SIR,—About two years ago you did me the favor to insert in the *Calcutta Gazette* a paper containing instructions for forming the then new philosophical instrument called the *galvanic pile*, and for performing some of the few experiments then known on the subject. Since that time galvanism has been continued to be cultivated, and with an activity unexampled in the annals of philosophy. The improvements and discoveries have been numerous and important. Who could suppose, for instance, that in so short an interval the power of the galvanic machine would have been so much increased as not only to ignite all sorts of inflammable substances, but also to melt, and even deflagrate all the metals, exhibiting a series of the most beautiful and striking experiments in philosophy? In short, who could possibly have imagined that a single pile, consisting of no more than *fifty series*, could produce effects superior to the united efforts of a dozen of the most powerful electrical machines yet constructed.

But as every discovery is, or at least ought to be, valued in proportion to the advantages which it can bring to society, the medical application of galvanism will, no doubt, claim the first attention of your readers.

From the first experiment of Galvani to the great discovery of Volta, including an interval of about nine years, few or no attempts were made to apply galvanism to medicine; the action of a single pair of metals, all that was then known, was so very feeble that no useful effect could rationally be expected from it. But on the discovery of the galvanic pile, and consequently of a mode of increasing the galvanic power in any proportion, physicians immediately set about applying this new discovery to the healing art. The consequence has been a number of remarkable cures performed by galvanism, and recorded by some of the most eminent medical characters in Europe. The following are some of the diseases in the cure of which galvanism has been completely successful. Acute rheumatism, paralytic affections, violent headaches, deafness, and what is more extraordinary than them all, two cases of melancholy madness, and one of confirmed hydrophobia. These, I am persuaded, will be sufficient to engage the attention of the medical gentlemen of this country. Many unsuccessful attempts must necessarily be made, and many failures may

I

naturally be expected. This has been the common lot of every new medicine. The physician who is animated with the true spirit of his profession will never permit a few unsuccessful cases to divert him from his object, particularly when he considers that he is treading a new and unbeaten path where, for anything he knows to the contrary, he may be already within grasp of a discovery which is to save the lives of thousands. To the usual motives to exertion, such as character, fame, emolument, &c., common to most professions, the physician has one peculiar to his own, which, in every well-conditioned mind, will operate as powerfully as any of the rest, and that is the heartfelt satisfaction of being the instrument sometimes of rescuing a fellow creature from the jaws of death. And a higher gratification than this I think the human mind can seldom enjoy. In what light the antient Romans,—many of whose civil institutions were founded in deep wisdom and sound policy,—considered this act, is sufficiently manifest from their well-known law, which ordained that the man who saved the life of a citizen should be permitted, ever after, to wear the civic crown. When this man entered the public theatre the whole assembly, consisting sometimes in the great theatres of forty or fifty thousand spectators, though in the middle, or most interesting part of the exhibition, stood up, and even the Senate, and in latter times the Emperors not excepted, unanimously saluted the wearer of the civic crown.

It may perhaps be asked—since galvanism and common electricity have been proved to be the same—what advantage can be expected from the one which may not be had from the other? The advantages in favour of galvanism are numerous. The following may suffice. Galvanism may be applied in an *uninterrupted* stream for several hours, whereas electricity acts in violent starts, and instantaneously. The galvanic apparatus is infinitely more portable than an electric machine. The former may be erected at home in ten or twelve minutes ; it may be carried in two small boxes in the pocket, if necessary, to the house of the patient, and in one minute may be ready for application. Again—the galvanic machine, consisting of strong solid plates of metal, is not liable to be out of order ; and lastly, it acts best in a moist atmosphere, and consequently may be employed during the rainy season, when no common electrical machine will act, a very important consideration in this country.

Having been the means of introducing galvanism to the notice of the public in this country, and having considerably improved the apparatus, I now take leave of the subject—I mean of medical galvanism—by resigning it into the hands of professional gentlemen, who alone are capable of ascertaining and fully appreciating its effects, and who, by a long series of experiments frequently repeated, will ultimately determine the real medical value of this extraordinary discovery. In medicine, particularly with respect to those diseases which have generally been found incurable, Lord Bacon's advice applies with equal propriety and force to physicians as well as philosophers,—*Fiat experimentum.*

Astronomy had always been a favorite science, which was continued to be cultivated in India. It was, however, often regretted that so few of the phenomena of the heavens had been observed, and no observations established from which to expect a regular series of labors. The occultations of the stars, visible in India, seldom occur in Europe ; eclipses and transits, too, happen under different phases, and without corresponding observations the labors of the astronomer lose half their value. It was from these circumstances the Doctor exerted himself in drawing the attention of scientific men throughout India to a useful and delightful study in a climate peculiarly favorable for its cultivation. Independent of his correspondence, communications were occasionally inserted in the papers to catch the public eye. The want of fixed instruments was much felt. In concluding an account of the then newly discovered planets, Ceres and Pallas, and alluding to the co-partnership entered into by the European astronomers for examining the heavens, he says, " I am sorry that the Bengal astronomers can contribute nothing to this great survey. Without an observatory all our efforts would be fruitless. I will even take the liberty of adding, that, without an observatory, neither the geography of this nor of any other country can ever become perfected."

Government had directed, from time to time, numerous surveys for the improvement of the geography of Hindostan, and during the important spherical survey by Major Lambton, the annexed letter was laid before the Supreme Council, but not honored with that attention its importance seemed to merit.

J. LUMSDEN, Esq.,
Chief Secretary to Government,

SIR,—Will His Excellency, the Most Noble the Governor-General in Council, pardon the liberty I take in suggesting what would, in my opinion, greatly contribute to the improvement of the geography and navigation of this country; that is, the erecting a small astronomical observatory at Calcutta.

It is certain that the longitude on land can be ascertained with precision only by corresponding observations, which cannot be taken and calculated by any *one* person, except with fixed instruments; that is, in an observatory.

I have said small observatory, for there is no occasion now for those large and expensive instruments which, in the infancy of modern practical astronomy, were necessary for settling the elements of the planetary motions, and at a time when mathematical instrument making was in a very imperfect state. The planetary motions are now ascertained to a degree of accuracy beyond which little can be either expected or wanted; and the mathematician has so much improved his art that astronomical instruments are made to perform as much now as those three times the size and price did formerly.

It would be the business of the astronomer to predict, observe, and register every useful celestial phenomenon, and instruct the gentlemen in the Company's service, as might require it, in the best mode of taking and working all such observations; also in such branches of the mathematical and philosophical sciences, as might be more immediately connected with their respective professions. It might also be part of his duty to regulate the numerous chronometers belonging to the Honorable Company's ships, a matter of considerable importance.

To the astronomical there might be added a meteorological apparatus, and a regular diary should be kept. From the more regular succession of the seasons, greater progress might be expected to be made in this most useful science here than in Europe.

Should this letter be honored with any attention by the Governor-General in Council, I am ready, if required, to make out an account of the various instruments requisite for both sciences, with their prices nearly; and from twenty-five years' almost constant experience, in both the theory and practice of a favorite science, I humbly hope that I shall be deemed not altogether unqualified to make out such a statement.—I am Sir,

Your most obedient servant,

Calcutta,   J. DINWIDDIE.
19 March, 1804.

On the subject of meteorology, above alluded to, the most enthusiastic feelings seem to have been entertained, as will be seen by the annexed critique:—

"In the third volume of the *Asiatic Researches* there is prefixed the following advertisement, by the President:

"*As it seemed proper to exhibit, at one view, the whole of Lieutenant Wilford's learned essay on Egypt and the Nile, there was not room in this volume for a meteorological journal; and it may be doubted whether the utility of such diaries compensates for their tediousness, and for the space which they occupy. The two specimens already published will give a correct idea of the weather in this part of India.*

"This relates to a meteorological journal kept by an ingenious gentleman of this settlement lately returned to Europe, and which had been inserted in the two preceding volumes of the *Researches* Did the very learned Sir William Jones really entertain any doubts respecting the utility of such diaries, or whether they were worth their room and the trouble of printing them? If knowledge be valuable in proportion to its advantages to society, a knowledge of the atmosphere must be the most useful of all the sciences. But such a knowledge is to be ascertained only by accurate diaries kept in every country on earth. When a sufficient number of observations shall have been made, the Almighty, in kind compassion to the wants of his children, will send another Newton into this world, who will collect the scattered observations, compare them together, and trace them up to a few, perhaps to one general cause from which the atmospherical phenomena will be explained, and its future changes will be calculated. I confess, I look forward with pleasure to that, though perhaps distant period, and were I possessed of the knowledge of all the antiquities of every country on earth, and from Adam to the present moment, I would willingly exchange the whole for the ability of predicting, but for twelve months, a tornado or hurricane in a West India island, or a bad seed-time or harvest at home. To the farmer, the merchant, and consequently to every description of men, such predictions would be of infinite importance.

"But I shall be told that the changes of the atmosphere seem to obey no fixed laws; that meteorological journals have been kept for many years, and nothing like a theory has yet been established; and that nature has thrown a veil over some of her works that man cannot remove. If after knowing that the phenomena of the solar system have been traced to *one* general law, will any man say that the atmospherical phenomena, of infinitely more importance to mankind, tumble into existence from the trembling hand of a blind fate? He may say so, but he will find no person credulous enough to believe what he cannot believe himself. From the present state of our knowledge of nature,—we may venture to affirm that she has no veil but what time's assiduous observation and persevering experiments may remove. That meteorological diaries have been kept for many years is certain; but how few the number, and how imperfect the register. It is only about twenty years since meteorology began to be cultivated as a science. It was then that Prince Charles Theodore, Elector Palatine of the Rhine, first established in his capital, Manheim, an academy for the sole purpose of meteorology. The transactions of that academy, of which the writer of this has the first to the fourth volume, do much honor both to the patron and superintendents of the institution. The importance of this science begins to be better known. The improved and happy revolutions in chemistry have enabled us to explain several of the subordinate phenomena of the atmosphere: and when we find such men as Kirwan, Playfair, Fourcroy, &c., applying this subject, what may we not hope for. A meteorological and astronomical apparatus may with great propriety be united, and the two sciences prosecuted in the same observatory. I intended to have subjoined to this a catalogue of instruments, with what I take to be the best form of a meteorological journal, but I have already taken up too much of your very interesting paper.

"It will not I hope be imagined, by what I have already said, that I mean to undervalue any branch of history, particularly one so entertaining as that of antiquities, and still more the labors of the gentleman mentioned in the advertisement, which, in the opinion of many readers, constitute the first ornament of the *Asiatic Researches*, and are read with the greatest avidity by every country in Europe. But however valuable these labors may be, their value, like that of everything sublunary, is *comparative*, and if put into the scale against the science I contend for, they would, in my opinion, '*kick the beam.*'"

The professorship proved the reverse of a sinecure, and the Doctor had serious obstacles to surmount in his exertions to diffuse science, which met with the greatest neglect from those who were to reap the benefit. Some remarks, at the conclusion of the third term of the second year, strikingly illustrate these facts.

" We have now finished an extensive system of scientific education; have employed two terms on natural philosophy, two on chemistry, and the same space of time on natural history. When I became connected with the college, I undertook the two branches of natural philosophy and chemistry—that of natural history was an afterthought. I hope, however, it has proved neither uninteresting nor uninstructive. That these lectures have been free from defects I never had the vanity either to affirm or believe; but, with the candid hearer, two circumstances, I think, should procure me some indulgence.

" First,—My particular situation at so great a distance from a glass work—the breakage in that way, which must always be considerable, can neither be repaired nor replaced. At the same distance from an operative chemist, and few chemicals to be had here, I have been under the necessity of preparing almost all the chemicals made use of; and you will readily agree with me, that to sweat over a furnace in a laboratory, in such a climate as this, is no very agreeable employment. The operator would require to be possessed of something more than mere good-will to the sciences.

" Another circumstance is,—that these lectures have been given by candle light, and consequently many experiments could not be rendered sufficiently visible, and many more could not be exhibited at all. This was no fault of mine, nor of any one else. Indeed, I am convinced that no hour more convenient than the present could have been adopted.

" With all their defects, however, I feel satisfied that these courses will, to the attentive student, serve as a sufficient foundation for his future studies—as a useful outline, the filling up of which will both usefully and agreeably employ many of the vacant hours of life. To every teacher of sensibility, the approbation of his pupils must afford the highest gratification, and to the gentlemen, who attended regularly, I beg leave to return my best thanks. To those of a different description, who favor us with a visit once a month—and I am sorry the number is much greater than I could possibly have expected—I shall only tell them that the time will come when they will regret having neglected the only opportunity which, in all probability, they will ever have of acquiring a knowledge of those most useful, elegant, and manly sciences.

" Before I conclude, I cannot help mentioning a circumstance that has exceedingly disappointed me. When I gave in to the College Council the plan of my philosophical courses, which was approved of, I could not suppose that there would be a sufficient number of proficients in mathematics to justify my introducing the theory along with the experimental part. It was therefore determined to give a merely experimental course, as a good foundation for theory at the next repetition. With this in view, in drawing up the heads of the lectures, I distributed the heads of the principal subjects of natural philosophy in the form of propositions, most of which are capable of theoretic as well as experimental proof; and as a teacher of mathematics had not then been appointed, my offers to teach that class also were accepted; but I am sorry to say, that, notwithstanding every effort of the College Council to establish a public class for mathematics, and frequent offers from myself to teach any gentlemen privately, not a single student has offered, and consequently we are no further advanced in the elements than when we at first commenced the practice."*

The benefit which the Doctor expected from joining the college was not to be realized. Much greater encouragement was given to other departments, particularly the oriental languages, for which it seems to have been alone instituted. His principal inducement in accepting the appointment was to effect a sale of the apparatus. On his first connexion with the college, and for many months afterwards, the Provost and Vice-Provost gave him to understand that it was *almost certain* Government would, in the end, purchase the whole for the use of the institution. With this in view, and little imagining that five hundred rupees a month would be deemed an adequate allowance for his services, different expensive investments were ordered from London, particularly in the glass line, by which not only the breakage of several years was repaired, but the whole collection made fit for every purpose of natural philosophy and chemistry. When three years had elapsed the state of his health was such as to cause him to think seriously of returning to Europe, and he was only prevented from resigning his situation on account of the apparatus, the disposal of which was absolute to the accomplishment of his wishes. A settlement of this question was then urged upon the College Council, and, in answer to a *resolution* from that body, the Doctor writes: "I herewith send a list of my apparatus, with the prices which I expect for them annexed. In valuing the instruments, I have been guided by the following rule: During my residence in this country I have sold a great number of instruments, similar to most of those in the list, the mean price of

---

* It would appear that in other departments of the college the same neglect was manifested by pupils, without, however, receiving the same disapprobation. We read : " *Degrees of honor* are marks of distinction bestowed on such students as are next to those who get medals and premiums. Mr. B. has recommended nine for Latin and Greek, several of whom never attended him."

the former I have chosen as a standard for the valuation of the articles in the list; and where the instrument has suffered by wear, though still useful, a proportionate reduction has been made in the price. The reasonableness of this mode will be obvious to, and I hope will meet with the approbation of the College. I now take the liberty of offering the apparatus to Government, and humbly request to know whether, on condition that the College Council shall be satisfied, Government will agree to take the apparatus at the end of the year, when I propose to resign my situation in the college."

After much delay, Government not only refused to take the apparatus, but also to make good the expenses incurred on account of the institution. The main objection urged against the purchase was the size of the collection, and the uncertainty of being provided with a successor sufficiently qualified to make a proper use of it. His resolution, however, to leave India was fixed, and, on the termination of his services in 1805, the Doctor began, by private bargain, to dispose of the whole collection, books, chemicals, and apparatus, reserving only a portion of his curiosities. The sale was attended with many difficulties, and progressed so slowly that his stay in the country was likely to be protracted much beyond his own desire. To make good his retreat, an agent was appointed to complete the sale and wind up his affairs, while he made all preparation for England.

The burning climes of the east had somewhat impaired a robust constitution; his anxiety to return was, nevertheless, natural in a man verging on sixty years far from all relations, or early friends. In all his wanderings, he never lost sight of his native land. In spite of philosophy, the *amor patriæ*—the remembrance of former friends, and former scenes—frequently stole over him with deep reflection on his advancing years, and urged him to spend at home the evening of an active life, which, probably, might wear out a little longer in his native air. He had acquired a handsome competency, though of all roads to wealth, that through the sciences seems the least direct; and notwithstanding his mind was never given to the accummulation of wealth. *

* When Dr. D. left England he was some £500 in debt, owing chiefly to about half-a-dozen well-to-do individuals, who had befriended him in his struggles, particularly in London. These he gradually cleared off while in India, or soon after his return to England, where he landed worth £10,000. Most of the money, however, remained in India, accumulating at a high rate of interest, which exceeded the demands upon it.

CHAPTER IX.

RETURN TO ENGLAND—DEATH.

THE passage for England had been engaged on board the Sir William
Pulteney, and on the 15th September, 1806, Calcutta was left for
good. In descending the Hoogly, to join the Sir William, which lay
a few miles below, and on the point of sailing, he had the mortification to find himself too late—the vessel was gone, all owing to want
of attention on the part of the boatmen, who should have started
some hours sooner. Among a variety of doubtful reports, it was
considered probable to overtake the Sir William, or some other vessel,
but the attempt was hazardous should the winds arise, which was not
at all unlikely. However, with much anxiety, the boatmen went to
work, and rowing hard for two successive days and nights, the Doctor
was safely placed in his own cabin, and through the most troublesome
part of a voyage homeward-bound. Some agreeable time was spent
at Madras and the Cape of Good Hope, beyond which little transpired to vary the monotony of the voyage, which terminated at
Blackwall, on the 15th April, 1807.

Home to him who has been long and far away is generally
attractive, as it proved to Dr. Dinwiddie, who arrived at a period
when the pursuit of knowledge seemed to merit the attention its
importance demanded. Institutions for the progress of science, or
the improvement of arts and manufactures, were rapidly rising into
existence all over the country. In the metropolis, the Royal, the
Surrey, and the London Institutions, were conspicuous; nor less the
Royal Academy, devoted to the fine arts alone. Such a wonderful
change could not but be satisfactory to the feelings of an individual
who had devoted his whole life to science. He had now given up
all intention of lecturing himself, but became a zealous supporter of
the lectures of others. The Royal and the Surrey Institutions were
the principal attractions, the former on account of Professor Davy's
brilliant operations by galvanism. But the zeal of Dr. Dinwiddie
carried him to attend every course of lectures within reach, if health
or prior engagements did not interfere. An unfortunate circumstance
occurred to lessen the pleasures derived from these and other sources.
Soon after his arrival, but from reasons not assigned, the sense of
hearing was lost to that degree that he was unable to distinguish the
beat of a watch applied to either ear. It somewhat recovered, but
his medical attendants in vain endeavored to remove the obstruction.
Still he seemed willing to console himself with the idea of having

enjoyed his hearing and other faculties so long. "At upwards of
sixty years of age, and after having spent fifteen years in the torrid
zone, good health is more than I can well expect." But on a subsequent occasion, he observes, " my want of hearing is so great an
inconvenience to me that I shall seldom dine abroad, and when I do,
avoid argument as much as possible."

On settling in London, one of his first objects was to fit up a study
for books and instruments, which he began to collect anew in order
to pass time, or amuse his friends. The rooms were besides stored
with a valuable collection of curiosities from China, India, and the
South Seas. Among them a mandarine's dress, made from the silk
presented by the Emperor of China, and a full set of Indian deities,
in marble, proved very interesting. The only business transactions
that he attended to was executing commissions for India, in the
mathematical, philosophical, and scientific line in general. This was
adopted as a light and agreeable recreation, and necessarily fixed his
residence to the metropolis, where he had a large connexion among
publishers and philosophical workmen. His long practice gave him
a decided superiority in executing such commissions, and so much
reliance was placed upon his experience by some friends in India,
that the captains had the strictest charges to receive no chests but
from the Doctor himself.

Bad health, in conjunction with other circumstances, prevented an
earlier visit to his friends, and relatives in the north, for which he
sailed on the 29th May, 1808. During his long absence, the country
had everywhere received astonishing improvements, but in no place
more than in Edinburgh, where a new town, more magnificent than
the old, had risen into existence between what used to be the North
Loch and the sea. The scenes of his early youth, which had not
been once visited since he commenced his professional career, nearly
thirty years ago, had been entirely changed. Large tracts, then in
a state of nature, were now sub-divided, and flourishing under a
system of cultivation hitherto unknown. Dumfries itself had shared
in the general improvement, nor was the faces of the inhabitants less
new than the streets and elegant buildings that embellished the
antient burgh. The fluctuation of human society was here experienced
in the most forcible manner. With a few exceptions, all his early
friends were dead, or removed to other places. Nevertheless, his
reception must have been very gratifying to his feelings. Invitations
flowed in upon him from many of the most respectable individuals,
and amongst others the families where he first commenced his career
of instruction. He had moreover the honor of dining in public with
the presbytery, and on another occasion with the magistrates of the

burgh. A galvanic apparatus, and a number of eastern curiosities, accompanied him as a source of amusement to his friends, who were ambitious of his residence being fixed amongst them; but this would have interfered with his arrangements in London, where he landed again in September following.

During the summer of the next year, a second excursion to Scotland was put into execution. A circumstance transpired on this occasion to bring about a misunderstanding with the authorities of Dumfries. On his previous visit to this place, Dr. Dinwiddie was curious to see the schools over which he formerly presided, and where he left behind him a small library of about three hundred and fifty volumes, and a philosophical apparatus, the latter chiefly belonging to a society of gentlemen subscribers, none of whom were now alive. The instruments were entirely neglected and out of order, which, with other circumstances, proved that no use would ever be made of them in the school-room, under the present arrangement. Still wishing to render at least the philosophical portion of the apparatus useful to the town, he requested permission to have the whole cleaned and repaired at his own expense. And besides, he intended to make such necessary additions to the apparatus as would render it fit for a full course of lectures on natural philosophy. It was, in short, his desire to establish a society at Dumfries, to which the library and apparatus should be presented, and the latter brought into a state of activity it had not enjoyed since 1777. The proposal met with a favorable reception from many gentlemen, both in town and country, and there seemed no doubt of the result being successful; but an opposition was raised by the mathematical teacher, and supported by the magistrates, who laid claim to the instruments, and frustrated the plan. The Doctor's feelings were much hurt by this circumstance, particularly when reflecting that the towns of Ayr, Perth, Dundee, Inverness, and probably several others in Scotland, had each an apparatus, and philosophical lectures given, not only to the youth, at their education, but occasionally to the public, while his native town, of not less importance, was wholly destitute of such advantages. The main objection urged was that *experiments took off the attention of the boys.* "I take the liberty of saying," observes the Doctor, "that experiments attract the attention to subjects of infinitely more importance to nine boys out of ten than all the mathematics that even Mr. White himself can teach them."

On the 6th July, 1810, Dr. Dinwiddie was elected a member of the Royal Institution, under its new act, and soon after placed on the Committee of Mathematics, Mechanics, and Mechanical inventions. At the conclusion of Singer's lectures on electricity, in this institution, April, 1811, the *British Neptune*, newspaper, giving an account of the proceedings, sums up in the following words: "The lecturer concluded this lecture to the general satisfaction of a numerous and highly respectable audience, among whom we noticed several men of science, and particularly one of the first and oldest popular lecturers (Dinwiddie) now living."

The effects of old age were fast increasing when the Doctor seriously began to reflect on his position in life, and the proper disposal of his effects. He appears to have made up his mind to spend the remainder of his days among his relatives in the north, and to breathe his last where his first breath was drawn. His apparatus, library, &c., were accordingly sent off to Scotland, followed sometime afterwards by himself, in company of a reverend friend, Dr. Scott of St. Michael's, Dumfries. They took the route by Oxford, spending a few days to inspect the various colleges and library of this celebrated seat of learning.

In Dumfries, with his son-in-law,* Dr. Dinwiddie took up his residence, and here as in London had apartments sufficiently ample to contain a library and philosophical room, where he continued to work experiments for the pure love of the facts which they furnished. His chief hobby was to draw the attention of his numerous friends and visitors to these objects. Unforeseen circumstances, however, conspired to break in upon the comforts which had been anticipated. Dumfries was evidently not what it used to be. He had been too long absent, and with the scientific recreations of the metropolis strongly in remembrance, he was induced to return, after an absence of exactly twelve months. Except the inconvenience to his hearing, he had enjoyed tolerable health, but from this time a daily alteration for the worse became visible. In the month of November, 1813, he was confined to his room, from which he never removed for the space of six months. During this period he was frequently subject to fainting fits, and on the evening of the 3rd April had no fewer than five attacks in the short space of two hours. His pulse would likewise make strange stops, losing one or two pulsations in succession. But even these matters were to him full of interest, and presented subjects for inquiry. On one occasion—when he had recovered from a fainting fit—his physician told him that his body was perfectly cold, and yet his pulse went regular. "This fact," remarked the Doctor, "is against Crawford's doctrine of animal

---

* Dr. D's only child was the wife of James Proudfoot, gunmaker, Dumfries, who eventually fell heir to most of the property, including books, pictures, instruments, and curiosities.

heat, and in favour of Brodie's, which derives it from the brain." He somewhat rallied in May following, but from this time seldom went abroad, and still less into society. Although his attendance at the Royal Institution was greatly fallen off, he was, nevertheless, on the 15th June, placed on the Committee of Chemistry, Geology, and Minerology. He took much interest in the success of this institution, and when unable to attend was anxious to know what was going forward. Once when the card of lectures was neglected to be sent, he felt quite hurt, and wrote for it. Even during his absence in Scotland, the cards were regularly forwarded to orders. By the advice of his physicians he removed to Pentonville, a more airy and healthy situation, but derived no particular benefit. Bad health continued to increase, and, after a short confinement, he expired on the 19th of March, 1815.* His remains were deposited in a leaden coffin, and buried in St. James' Church, Pentonville, where they rest without the slightest memorial to mark the spot.

❋   ❋   ❋   ❋   ❋   ❋

* In a note to stanza 47, Mayne's "Siller Gun," will be found a brief memoir of Dr. D., who is said to have "died on the 15th March, 1815." The 15th is either a typographical error, or a small mistake of the author: the memoir, however, is substantially correct, and is as follows:—"This gentleman was celebrated not only for his talents and scientific acquirements, but for his mild and inoffensive manners. In early life he pursued the honorable career of a teacher of youth, and for many years filled the office of preceptor of the mathematical school of Dumfries, to which he was appointed in November, 1771. Accounted one of the most eminent literary and scientific characters then in Dumfries—and these were not a few—he was enabled to found there perhaps the first literary debating society for philosophical and moral discussions of which Dumfries could boast. The society was composed partly of his own pupils, students, and gentlemen of talent, of whom each might offer his opinion on a given question or subject, supporting it by such arguments as he thought proper. Dr. D. afterwards distinguished himself as a public lecturer in various branches of science, in which capacity he visited the principal cities of the British Empire. Having attracted the notice of Lord Macartney, he was selected by that nobleman to accompany him in his embassy to China, as astronomer and superintendent of the mathematical instruments intended as presents to the Emperor. He had previously received the degree of LL.D. in the University of Edinburgh. After discharging the duties of his appointment to the entire satisfaction of his superiors, Dr. D. proceeded to India, where he was further honored by the present Marquis Wellesley, who nominated him Professor of Natural and Experimental Philosophy in the splendid college of Fort William, which had just been established. Here Dr. D. spent many happy years, esteemed and respected by all who knew him, and returned, after acquiring a moderate competence, to pass the remaining part of his life in his native country. His health, however, had suffered from the vicissitudes of climate to which he had been for a long period exposed, but his faculties exhibited all the energy of a strong mind to the last.—JOHN MAYNE."

Thus lived and died Dr. James Dinwiddie—devoting a long life to the accumulation and diffusion of scientific knowledge. Beyond transitory communications in the newspapers, chiefly in India, he never risked his reputation as an author. On this point he had a delicacy, which was greatly augmented by the want of leisure to digest and write his observations methodically. He left, however, a large collection of papers behind him. At the time of his death, these papers fell into the hands of one of his executors, a merchant in Old Broad Street, where they lay buried some forty years before they came into the hands of the present possessor, mutilated, corroded, and otherwise disfigured. Originally, they embraced many documents now wholly missing. In their present abused state, there is, in the first place, an extensive correspondence with scientific men: There is "A course of Lectures on Natural Philosophy and Chemistry," showing their influence on the daily occupations of life: there is another extensive course on "Natural History;" another on the "Fine Arts;" and another on "Antient and Modern War:" there is an "Essay to determine the true order of battle among the Antients;" a large collection of "Miscellaneous Papers," embodying Reports and observations on manufactures and machinery: there are upwards of twenty small volumes of "Queries and Hints;" several similar volumes of "Nugæ, Anecdotes, and Literary subjects;" "Journal through China;" "Journal in India," &c., &c.

FINIS.

COPIES

ORIGINAL LETTERS

QUOTED IN, OR FURNISHING INFORMATION FOR, THIS WORK.

[October, 1778.]

DEAR SIR,—I was unluckily from home when your letter arrived, so that I did not receive it till some time after its date. I am very happy to hear of your success in the different courses you have given, and hope it will induce you to give us next summer some instruction in Ayr. You will be so good as deliver the enclosed to Mr. Playfair when you go to Dundee. He lives about two miles from the town, and I am sure will be glad to see you at his manse. Could you order matters so as to pay us a visit at Catrine in your way back to Dumfries?

I am, dear Sir,

Your most obedient Servant,

To Mr. JAMES DINWIDDIE,   DUGALD STEWART.

Skinner's Close, Edinburgh.

SIR,—My passion for philosophical studies, and the necessity of carrying my apparatus and lectures to a degree of perfection equal to any of my predecessors, or contemporaries, together with Mr. Tennent's abilities and application, form the only apology I can make to the town council of Dumfries for my not returning at Whitsunday last. The first cost plunged me into a debt of a hundred and fifty pounds. To pay off this, the only scheme that carried probability of success was that of giving public lectures. The indulgence of the magistrates and council of Dumfries enabled me to put this in execution; and the approbation of my friends encouraged me to go on. My success has been much greater than, from my little experience and want of that confidence so necessary for pushing on through the world, I had reason to expect. My ambition to excel in my favorite study swells with my apparatus, and I have advanced so far that I now find it impossible to retreat. I flatter myself, however, that, though I have not literally fulfilled my obligations to the town council, I have not acted contrary to the spirit of them. I have not drawn a farthing from the school since last Whitsunday, Mr. Tennent having deservedly enjoyed both the salary and emoluments. As my connexion with the school is now only nominal, and as the continuance of it can be no longer of use, either to the town of Dumfries or to myself, I request the favor that you will be pleased to signify to the magistrates and council this my resignation of the mathematical school of Dumfries, with my most grateful acknowledgement for all their favors. It affords me some consolation to think that my favorite studies, which I had the honor first to establish in Dumfries, are to be carried on, with every improvement that modern discoveries may suggest, by Mr. Tennent, of whose abilities and application you have had the best of all possible proofs—above two years' experience. The few instruments in my custody belonging to the subscribers shall be replaced with new ones, which I have ordered some time ago, with such additions to their collection as the subscribers, I am confident, will acknowledge to be a sufficient equivalent for the use of the small part of their apparatus which I have had along with me. The papers containing the receipts I granted for every farthing I received of their money—are in the hands of some of the gentlemen who collected the money. Along with this apparatus I will send a catalogue of the whole collection, that the subscribers may be sensible how their money has been expended.

My warmest wishes shall ever attend the mathematical school of Dumfries. I hope to have it yet in my power to return the many obligations I am under to the magistrates and council and to the town in general.

I am, Sir,
Your much obliged humble servant,
JAS. DINWIDDIE.

THOS. BOYD, Esq.,   Cork, 4 Nov., 1780.
    Dumfries.

[Dublin, 1782.]

MY DEAR SIR,—The sensations your letter excited in my breast, you will easily judge of from those of your own. My affliction is greatly augmented from the consideration of the neglect with which I have treated many of my friends, and particularly my dear friend whose situation puts it out of my power to make any compensation. But why trouble you with such reflections? Necessity compelled me to this wandering life. I offered my apparatus to the town, at least privately to some friends in the council, at the prime cost, discounting the expense of two jaunts to London I was obliged to take in order to purchase them, but was told the town would not agree to it. What could I do? The only thing left was lecturing. Though my success in this way was pretty tolerable, yet I soon found that, to please the giddy and unthinking who compose the greater part of every audience, considerable additions were from time to time requisite. After travelling from one end of this kingdom to the other, I returned to Dublin with ninety-six pounds. I had paid a considerable part of my debts, and part of the above sum was intended to defray the remainder, when a merchant, who professed for me the greatest friendship, and who was generally understood to be in a good way, contrived to borrow it of me. He immediately stopped! You may judge of my situation. This happened a little before Mr. Tennent was in Dublin, at which time I had not a single guinea in my pocket. The drawing of the Irish lottery had occasioned a stagnation in every kind of business I now for the first time experienced the want of money in a strange country. In this dilemma, after many schemes formed in my own breast—for even my cousin knew not my situation—I accidentally met with a *Scotch* gentleman, who told me he had a son at a school where a course of geography was much wanted. I agreed to walk *three* miles to this school three days in the week, for ten guineas the first quarter, which the master engaged to pay. This, by an unexpected addition to the school, turned out twenty guineas. The next, which I have just finished, amounts to twenty-five. The parents are so much pleased with the progress of the boys, that the lectures in town are now better attended. I am in the receipt of about £180 a year: it will soon be more, but I now intend to settle in Ireland. I return my most grateful thanks to my friends in Dumfries for their kind remembrance of me. I prefer Dumfries to every other place, but I am sorry I cannot at present accept of it; I am engaged with this school for a twelvemonth, but there is a way by which my return to Dumfries may be probably brought about. However, as it is near twelve, and the post going, I must defer this plan, which offers a sufficient apology, for three posts.

I am, yours, &c.,

Mr. WM. KELLOCK,   JAS. DINWIDDIE.
       Dumfries.

P.S.—Can you send me a frank?

SIR,—I happened to be at Bristol when the man you sent called for the half-guinea, and having forgot to leave proper orders with my landlord—it was on this account not paid. I have now lodged a guinea and a half with Mr. Meyler, bookseller, in the Grove, Bath, which will be paid on delivery of the balloon. I am giving a course of lectures on Experimental Philosophy here; the possession of the balloon is on this account, at present, of more consequence to me than its real value. If any gentleman in your place chooses to have a small balloon, or indeed one of any size, I will engage to construct it cheaper and better than any man in England, having just discovered a composition by which the silk can be made perfectly air-tight, which has never yet been the case. The materials must come from London. I shall pay the expense of carriage.

I am, Sir, your humble servant,

JAMES DINWIDDIE.

Mr. WM. BALL, Shaftsbury.   Bath, 26th Jan. 1784.

Edinburgh, August 18th, 1792.

DEAR SIR,—I have the pleasure to inform you that the University of Edinburgh promoted you to the degree of LL.D. on Monday the 13th inst. Your diploma is written, and as soon as it is subscribed by the Principal, and such of the Professors as are in town, it will be forwarded by the mail coach in the way you have directed, so that you may expect to receive it in a few days. In the meantime you may consider yourself as certainly a Doctor as if you had the diploma in your custody, and may announce it in the London papers if you think proper.

It was with great pleasure the University conferred this mark of respect on an old alumnus, who has distinguished himself so much as you have done, particularly in natural science. I have no doubt that you will continue to distinguish yourself in another quarter of the world, and contribute your share to the lustre of a mission so worthy the dignity of the British nation.

Be so good as present my best compliments to Sir George Staunton, with whom I had the honor to be a little acquainted when he was in Edinburgh. Also to Mr. Huttner, the tutor of his son, a gentleman for whom I have a

K

great respect, having spent some agreeable hours with him in classical and philological conversation when he was here.

Believe me to be with great regard, Dear Sir,

Your most obedient humble servant,

JAMES DINWIDDIE, LL.D.,   ANDREW DALZELL.

No. 17, Great Suffolk Street,
Haymarket, London.

DEAR COUSIN,—I have two friends who accompany Lord Macartney in his Embassy to China, and are to touch at Madras. These gentlemen are Dr. Dinwiddie, Astronomer, &c, to the Embassy, and Mr. Chapman, one of the officers of the Lion. I trust you will pardon the freedom I take in strongly recommending them to your friendship, which you will find them in all respects most worthy of. Dr. Dinwiddie, as a man of science and a gentleman, does honor to his country; and Mr. Chapman's nautical abilities and private worth do credit to his Majesty's quarter deck. These gentlemen are on the point of sailing, I cannot therefore send you the interesting news from Europe, but am happy to introduce to your acquaintance persons well qualified to give you every information you can wish.

The present embassy to China has for its object the extension of trade, and a more intimate connexion between the Chinese and the British empires. The presents are most honorable to this country. Instead of diamond snuff-boxes, and other things of imaginary value, they consist of a most splendid collection of machinery for illustrating the various sciences, arts, and manufactures of Great Britain. But as Dr. Dinwiddie has the superintendence of the whole, and is to exhibit the various experiments, I refer you to him, who will have great pleasure in explaining to you the whole.

I have but time to add that I am, with the utmost gratitude and respect, my dear Cousin,

Your most affectionate friend,

And very humble servant,

WALTER MOWBRAY.

GEORGE MOWBRAY, ESQ.,
Accountant-General to the East   Portsmouth, 23 Sept., 1792.
India Company, Madras.

[1793.]

MY LORD,—The erecting and regulating the planetarium; the constructing, filling, and ascending in the balloon; the diving-bell; experiments in electricity, air, mechanics, and other branches of experimental philosophy; astronomical and other calculations—these I have all along considered as my province in the Embassy. I have accordingly been employed during the voyage in making such necessary calculations as could be made previous to being on the spot, and which I shall have the honor of submitting to your Excellency in due time.

Pardon me, my Lord, in observing that the term *machinest*, however it may be explained, will convey to a Chinese no other idea than that of a mechanic; and that the term mechanic but ill accords with the feelings of a man who has dedicated his whole life to mathematics and natural philosophy. Permit me humbly to request that your Excellency will substitute *mathematician,* instead of *machinist,* to the Embassy. The term, in the acceptation of the Chinese, is fully expressive of my whole business in the Embassy; it is a title which does not interfere with that of any other gentleman; and I humbly hope that twenty years' almost constant application to the theory and practice of mathematics, and with great goodwill to the subject, will excuse my applying for a title which I have borne for many years past.

Translated Extract of a Letter received in Canton from a Missionary at Pekin.

In the meantime, to comply with your desire, I will tell you a few things respecting the English Embassy.

Never did any embassy deserve better—not only on account of the experience, abilities and friendly character of Lord Macartney and Sir George Staunton, but also with respect to the talent and careful comportment of the whole suite, not to omit the rich and uncommonly costly and curious presents for the Emperor; yet notwithstanding all these (astonishing to relate) never had an embassy worse success than this.

The objects which the Court of London and the English East India Company had in view were to obtain:—

1st.—Leave for an English resident at Pekin, in order to keep a watchful eye on the trade of his nation.

2nd.—An establishment at Chusan, a small island 18 miles from Nimpo.

3rd.—A free trade to every port in the empire.

4th.—Commissioners in each province of the empire.

5th.—A tariff consisting of five defined regulations or laws respecting the customs at Canton, in opposition to the arbitrary mandates of the mandarines.

All these points were proposed in different conferences, both verbally and in writing, and were all answered and rejected—some simply without any further notice, others with remarks not very honorable, not to say insulting or offending.

As to the presents for the Emperor—Lord Macartney, who wished to stay at Pekin till March the next year, announced that he did not mean to offer them all at once, but at three different periods, for which purpose he had divided them into three different classes. The two first were offered and accepted by the Emperor. These consisted of superfine English broad-cloth of various colors; twenty-two books filled with chosen prints, curious hardware and stationery, an electrifying machine, a pneumatic machine, some pocket barometers, a large burning glass or mirror, two superb crystal crowns, whose balloquies (pyramids) reflect the colors of the rainbow, two coaches or chariots, two chairs with inside springs by which they follow and answer all the motions of the person sitting in them, and a most curious planetarium, whereon thirty years of labour have been bestowed. The third class of presents was never offered, as no time was given for it; for to everybody's astonishment, the Chinese Minister, who was charged by the Emperor with everything relating to the Embassy, after having delivered to the Ambassador the Emperor's presents, which are said not to be very costly, made him depart, with all his suite, in great haste, nearly in the same manner as I was sent away from Canton, without granting to his Excellency an audience of leave, or even leave to take a proper view of Pekin, nor to us to pay a single visit to his Excellency. Orders had also been sent before to all European missionaries not to come near the palace of the Ambassador. Such are the extraordinary scenes which have been exhibited on the theatre at Pekin, and which cannot fail to make a great noise in Europe and somewhere else.

You will perhaps be curious to know the reasons of such an uncommon and unfavorable conduct of the Chinese Government—I shall explain them to you in a few words:—

These gentlemen, as well as all those who do not know China but from books, were ignorant of the customs, usages, and etiquette of the court; and, to make bad worse, they brought with them a Chinese interpreter who knew still less of those matters, and whose fault it was that they never could obtain leave to have a European missionary with them, who could have instructed and directed them. The consequence thereof was:—

1st.—That they arrived without bringing any presents for the Ministers of State, and the sons of the Emperor.

2nd.—That they failed in the customary manner of the country to show their respect to the Emperor, without being able to assign any good reason for it.

3rd.—That they have been presented in their simple and common dresses.

4th.—That they have not taken care to fill the hands of those who had the charge of their persons and things; and

5th.—That in their written representation, they did not adopt the style and manner of the country.

Another, and, in my opinion, the principal cause of the ill success, has been the influence of a certain missionary, who, afraid of this Embassy becoming prejudicial to the trade of his countrymen, did his utmost to spread very disadvantageous reports of the English nation.

Add to all this that the Emperor is very old and extremely broken in health, and that in all countries are self-interested cabals and cunning subjects, whilst all the great ones and favorites of the Emperor only look out for prospects and riches.

———— ———

To Dr. Dinwiddie.

Sir,—The Governor-General has received letters from Lord Macartney, in which his Lordship mentions that he had put under your care some boxes of tea plants, and some plants of the varnish and tallow trees, which his Lordship had been so good as to procure during his journey from Pekin to Canton, and I am directed to request that they may be delivered to Dr. Roxburgh, the superintendent of the Company's Botanical Garden in this country, with any information it may be in your power to give him of their present state, and the best means of preserving them.

Lord Macartney having also acquainted the Governor-General that he had desired your care of some eggs of the China silk worm, I have orders to signify to you the wish of Government that these may be given to the Board of Trade.

I am, Sir,

Your most obedient, humble servant,

Council Chamber,　　　　　　　　　　　　　　　　E. HAY,
　　29th of Sept., 1794.　　　　　　　　　　　Sec. to Government.

LETTERS. **133**

To Dr. Dinwiddie.

Sir,—The Board of Trade being desirous of knowing the different degrees of goodness of the saltpetre manufactured in the provinces of Behar, Benares, and Oude, they desire you will please to examine and report to them their comparative qualities. Some of each sort you will be supplied with by the export warehouse-keeper.

I am, Sir,

Your most obedient, humble servant.

Fort William,   W. A. EDMONSTONE,
  the 8th September, 1795.   Sec. to Board of Trade.

Madras, 27th February, 1796.

Dear Sir,—The fleet sails to-morrow. I avail myself of this opportunity to write a few lines. Since I had the pleasure of writing you last, about twelve months ago, by Mr. Devis, I have been engaged in making experiments of somewhat greater magnitude than can be exhibited in a lecture room. The exorbitant price of vitriolic acid, in Bengal, had hitherto been a great drawback to the indigo and other manufactures. I proposed to Mr. Fairlie, one of the first merchants here, to erect works, and instruct any person he choosed in the mode of making the acid. The proposal was accepted of, and the works completed in three months. Our first attempt consisted of one hundred pounds of acid, equal to any made in England, and which can be sold at one-fourth the usual Bengal price. The real expense of the works turned out less than my estimate by at least one third. I intend to follow this up with the nitrous acid, and one or two other chemical articles procurable here at a very high price, and frequently with great difficulty. Our new manufacture of cochineal thrives astonishingly, and will, I hope, soon render the importation of that drug from Mexico unnecessary. I was employed by the Governor-General in Council to examine the Bengal cochineal; I find it of the second, or Silvestris kind, but pretty high in that class. The coloring matter is equal in *quality* to the very best Spanish mestique, with which I compared it, and the quantity of coloring matter was to that of the mestique as 10 to 19. It must be observed that the musters I used were insects reared during the *heavy rains*. I have no doubt but the size of the insect, and consequently the quantity of coloring matter, will, by proper cultivation, be much increased. There is no article of cultivation better adapted to the natural indolence of the native inhabitants than this; and perhaps no country in the world where the plant, to which the insect has taken, is found in greater abundance.

I have made several experiments lately on saltpetre, and am not without hopes of making some improvements in this manufacture. If I succeed in this, one boiling, at least, will be saved, and the saltpetre will be purer. In short, there is in this country an extensive field for the application of mechanism and chemistry to arts and manufactures. An agricultural and mineralogical survey would, I am persuaded, be productive of valuable discoveries. I am as busy as my situation will permit in collecting curious and useful information. I attend all the processes of the natives in refining of gold and silver, in which they excel; in spinning, weaving, bleaching, dyeing, &c., their different cloths; with every other art and manufacture that I can hear of. I have lately met with a valuable collection of the Hindoo gods in marble, well executed. I shall have models of all the most curious native machinery. My Sanscrit friends, particularly Mr. Wilford, promises to mark such passages in the antient writings as relate to chemistry, art, and manufactures of former ages ; though, to be plain with you, I am more anxious to know what the Hindoos are doing, and can do, at *present*, than what they were doing two thousand years ago. Mr. Samuel Davis, our antique astronomer, has made an *unfortunate* discovery lately—viz., he has found in one of the most antient Hindoo maps of the heavens, and in the southern hemisphere too, the constellation *Charles' Oak*. Believe me, this is fact, and has not a little perplexed our Asiatic Society, of which I have the honor to be a member, and where I have taken the liberty of recommending some attention to the *present times*. The last mentioned discovery has afforded me some advantages over my antique friends, and may be very satisfactorily accounted for, but this on some future occasion.

Mr. Wilford told me about two months ago that he had received some queries from Mr. Bruce, but from his having confined himself entirely to geography, he must apologise for not answering them. He added that I was, in his opinion, in a more favorable situation for collecting information than any other person in India. I humbly think that if such a survey as I have already mentioned were to take place, and I had an opportunity of visiting the different provinces, much useful information might indeed be collected. But without travelling in the Company's service, with respect to myself, it would be impossible. I have been informed that Sir. J. Shore has written in my favor to the court of directors, and also that some friends here have mentioned me to some of the directors. A habit of examining manufactures for nearly twenty years past at home, has given me much experience, and the possession of a large apparatus enables me to perform every necessary experiment. I am, at Madras, only on a visit, and return to Calcutta in the course of three or four weeks.

My London friends have all forgot me: I have had but one letter since my arrival in Bengal. At Pulo Penang, I picked up two plants of the elastic-gum tree. They are now flourishing in the Company's gardens at Calcutta. The bread-fruit tree also abounds in the Asiatic islands.

The only good mathematician I have met with, in this country, is a native, the Nabob of Oude's vakeel—his name Tuffoz-ul-Hussien. He is well-known to Mr. Hastings, who sends him out mathematical books. He has translated Newton's Principia into Arabic ; also Maclaurin's Fluxions, and the uncouth Emerson's Mechanics. He has been a constant attendant on me since my arrival in Bengal, and is extremely pleased to see the application of theory to practice. Of the latter he had not the least knowledge.

I am happy to hear that the long-expected regulations for the army are at length arrived, or at least certain intelligence that they will soon arrive. Matters were carried to an alarming length. The best informed men in this country were of opinion that the most serious consequences *must* take place, and wondered at the so long procrastination of the court of directors. The Sepoys declared they would, to a man, stand by their officers. The officers told them, from time to time, that they were to be commanded by King's officers—young boys unacquainted with their customs and their religion—arguments of sufficient weight to impose on a mind of greater strength than that of an honest, simple Sepoy.

I am, dear Sir,
Your most obedient servant,
J. DINWIDDIE.

To Joseph Hume, Esq.,
  Chemist, Long Acre, London.

To PETER SPEKE, Esq., President, &c., Members of the Board of Trade.

GENTLEMEN,—I duly received your secretary's letter of the 2nd August, transmitting copy of the letter, and of the instructions furnished by Dr. Dinwiddie, for erecting conductors for lightning on this factory.

The instructions are very clear and intelligible, and I should have no difficulty in following them were the workmen here competent to the task of making the iron and other metal materials required in a proper manner, which I believe they are not. I would beg leave therefore, gentlemen, to recommend the preparation of these articles in Calcutta, where they can be well made, and, I should suppose, cheaper, by being committed to the immediate direction of Dr. Dinwiddie, who has, I understand, already constructed some conductors there on the same plan. I have conversed with that gentleman on the subject of those to be erected here, and he is of opinion that the iron rods being made each of separate pieces, with strong screws, and to be united here afterwards, may be equally efficacious with rods of one entire piece of iron, which will facilitate their conveyance hither.

I have the honor to be, &c.,

G. UDNY,

Malda, 16th November, 1796. Resident.

To Dr. DINWIDDIE.

SIR,—Government having desired the Military Board to inspect and report on the state of the machinery and manufacture of gunpowder at Pultah, and the board conceiving that your knowledge in the theory of mechanics would be, on this occasion, of use to them, I am directed to intimate their request that, should you not have any objections, you will be so good as to meet them at the powder works near Pultah, early on the morning of Thursday the 17th inst., to assist them in their examination and report on the works and manufactory.

I am, Sir,

Your most obedient, humble servant,

ISAAC HUMPHREYS,

Military Board Office, Sec. Military Board.
9th July, 1800.

London, 16th November, 1807.

DEAR DAVID,—I have just received the papers from the India House. I learn from Joseph that the gongs, gods, and like articles are sold at the public sale, and pay 50 per cent. duty. I wish therefore to have those I left with you sent home. I should also be much obliged to you to get the names of the gods affixed to them. Mr. Bentley, or Mr. Forster, will probably do me this favor. If it be necessary to apply to a Brahmin, your sircar will no doubt find one for the purpose, whom you will pay. On account of the great weight of the images, it will probably be best to pack them and the gongs in *two* boxes. As they are part of my apparatus, Mr. Scott will probably let them pass free of duty; if not, pay the duty. I will thank you to send me two or three copies of my analysis. If there are none left with you, they may be had from Messrs. Lathrop and Phillot, or Mr. Carey. I will also thank you for Solvyn's pamphlet, which describes his large book of prints, and a quantity of *sola*, the light wood employed by fishermen in your river, to float their nets. Let it be of various sizes, both in length and thickness. It will serve to pack the gods, which must be made so fast as not to move when the box is upset. Mr. Fairlie made me a present of the gods upwards of ten years ago, on condition that if they were claimed by the owner, I was to return them. As this has not been done, I consider them as my own property.

Let me know whether the paper on galvanism, which I sent you from Saugur, was inserted in the *Calcutta Gazette*, and if so, whether there have been any remarks made on it. Galvanism here is throwing much light on several branches of chemistry.

I am, dear David,

Yours, &c.,

DAVID HARE, ESQ, Calcutta.   JAMES DINWIDDIE.

Dumfries, 11th September, 1809.

SIR,—On my leaving Dumfries in 1777, I left in the mathematical school a philosophical apparatus, with a small library containing about 350 volumes, for the use of that school, till I should return. On my return to Dumfries last year my intention was to present the apparatus, with some necessary additions, to the town of Dumfries, when proper rooms could be prepared for it in the new schools. This I had the pleasure of mentioning to you, Sir, last year. On inspecting the instruments at the mathematical school, I found that a complete repair was absolutely necessary. While I was considering how this might be best effected, I learned that James Proudfoot, whom I knew to be an ingenious mechanic, was about to settle in Dumfries. When this took place at Whitsunday last, Mr. White, at my request, let Proudfoot have a few instruments to repair, which he has done in so complete a manner as to prove that he can accomplish the whole. In consequence of this I applied to Mr. White for the remainder of the instruments, which were refused on the following grounds,—that he (Mr. White) had, on his settling in Dumfries, granted a receipt to the town for the apparatus, which receipt must be returned before parting with the apparatus. How the magistrates of Dumfries could demand a receipt for instruments which never belonged to the town can be accounted for only from their not being acquainted with the real history of the apparatus, which I shall endeavor to give in as few words as possible.

About the year 1772, Dr. George Chapman set on foot a subscription for a philosophical apparatus for the use of the town of Dumfries. The subscription paper contains about seventy to seventy-five pounds, one-half of which, however, was never *paid.* It appears from the subscription paper, which is in my bureau in London, that the town of Dumfries did not subscribe a shilling to the apparatus, and so far from its being intended that the instruments should be the property of the town, it is expressly declared in the preamble to the subscribers' names, "that the apparatus shall be kept in such a situation as a *majority of the subscribers shall determine.*" From this it will appear that the transaction is not with the town, but between the subscribers and me. Had Mr. White mentioned the circumstance of the receipt to me last year, the business might then have been settled in five minutes, for I had the subscription paper in my pocket. This paper was shown to some of my friends here, and particularly to Mr. Thomas Boyd, who is better acquainted with this business than any man now living.

I now take the liberty of requesting that the magistrates and council of Dumfries will be so obliging as to order the receipt to be returned to Mr. White ; or, if that be now impracticable, that they will release Mr. White from any obligation which such a receipt may be supposed to infer. This is all that Mr. White requires, and it is certainly what he has a right to. My intention is to put the whole apparatus into the hands of James Proudfoot, who, in the intervals of his business, will be able to put it into repair by next summer, when I shall consider of the best method of applying it to the use of the town, and of putting it in a state of activity which it has not enjoyed these thirty years.

It will not, I hope, be supposed, from what I have said, that I mean to throw any reflections on your mathematical teacher. Mr. White ranks among the first mathematicians of the age, and from the examination of his school last year, with other documents in my possession, I am certain that he is a most successful teacher. If he and I differ in opinion with respect to the great utility of the experimental sciences, this may be easily accounted for. For thirty years past I have been wholly engaged in cultivating these sciences, while Mr. White has, for a considerable part of the said time, been employed in the duties of your mathematical school, which he has discharged with much utility to the public and great credit to himself.

I am, Sir, with much respect,

Your most obedient humble servant,

DAVID STAIG, ESQ.,   J. DINWIDDIE.
Provost of Dumfries.

———

London, 19th February, 1812.

DEAR SIR,—The enclosed paper contains my mode of settling the apparatus business, which I doubt not that you will think liberal on my part. The subscribers themselves, *to whom alone I am accountable*, were they in life, must think so. I beg that you will get the two receipts exchanged—mine from the town, and theirs from Proudfoot. Tell Proudfoot to return the theodolite, for I have now nothing to do with the repairs of it.

In Tennant's list, a number of other articles are mentioned, such as Wilson's microscope, two parallel rulers, long legged compasses, double cone and inclined plane, &c. I expect to show you the list next summer, when I intend, if health permit, to visit Dumfries. I hope, however, that this foolish business will be settled first. Our friend Commissioner White may again conjure up the ghost of another receipt given to Mr. Aiken, or some other *defunct*, to puzzle us all. That Mr. White must have mistaken the receipt for some other given for a different purpose, I am fully convinced, and that Mr. Aiken was the *last man* among the subscribers who would have demanded a receipt for the apparatus *in behalf of the town*, I shall prove to you when we meet. I confess I left Dumfries last, a little out of humour at this business, and am afraid I did not behave with proper respect to Mr. Staig on that occasion. From that gentleman I have always received the most kind and polite attention, which it is impossible for me ever to forget.

On my visit to Dumfries in 1808, my intention was to get the apparatus repaired, and make such additions to it as were necessary for a full course of natural philosophy. But on seeing the state of the instruments, and on hearing Mr. White say (which he did in the little apparatus room) that *experiments took off the attention of the boys*, I was convinced that no use would ever be made of the philosophical part of the instruments, nor any lectures ever be given by him in the mathematical school of Dumfries. Still wishing to render the apparatus useful to the town, I requested Mr. White to let James Proudfoot have the instruments to clean and repair. He let him have a part, which, on my next visit in 1809, I found he (Proudfoot) had repaired, several at least, as well as I expected. When Proudfoot applied for the remainder of the instruments, Mr. White refused, on account of the *receipt to Mr. Aiken.* I thought of trying to establish a society at Dumfries, to which I should have made a present of the apparatus. From the favorable reception the proposal met with from several gentlemen, both in town and in the country, I had no doubt of success, though Mr. White told me a sufficient number could not be had. From Mr. White's opposition, and which seemed to be supported by the magistrates, I determined never again to trouble them on this, or perhaps *any other subject.* I confess I am much hurt when I think that the towns of Ayr, Perth, Dundee, Inverness, and probably several others in Scotland, have each an apparatus, and philosophical lectures given, not only to the youth at their education, but occasionally to the public, while my native town, of not less importance than most of the above, is wholly destitute of such advantages. Mr. White says that *experiments take off the attention of the boys.* I take the liberty of saying that experiments attract the attention to subjects of infinitely more use to nine boys out of ten, than all the mathematics that even Mr. White himself can teach them.

I promised to Mr. F. Short, when here, to write to him on this business, supposing then that you would not recover. But now that you have left the undertaker in the lurch, I trouble you, agreeably to a former compact between us, to settle the business, with which you are better acquainted than any other man living. Communicate this, with my compliments, to Mr. Short. I would have shown him both Tennant's and the non-payment lists, but was not so fortunate as to meet with Mr. S. till at the St. Paul's Coffee House, a few minutes before he stepped into the carriage for Scotland.

I am, dear Sir,

Yours very truly,

THOMAS BOYD, ESQ., Dumfries.   J. DINWIDDIE.

EDWARD HOWELL, LIVERPOOL.